ADVANCE PRAISE FOR
WOMEN WHO WIN AT LOVE

"Ms. Venker's contribution to humanity, to families, to marriages, to women is huge."
— Dr. Laura Schlessinger, author of six *New York Times* bestsellers and host of one of the most popular talk show hosts in radio history

"Suzanne Venker and John M. Townsend, Ph.D. positively implode the concept of sexual equality in this bold and courageous book. One explosive statement after another about sex, love, dating, and desire. Bam. Bam. Bam. Finally, America can have a conversation about the sexes that's devoid of gender propaganda. It's about time."
— Rebecca Hagelin, *Washington Times* columnist and author of *30 Days to Strengthen Your Family*

"If you are a woman and you want to be happy, read this book. Chances are, nobody has told you the truth inside that will transform your life. I've seen so many people, including me, learn what Suzanne and John write about through sometimes irreversible heartbreak. You don't have to if you learn from the timeless wisdom about men and women that Suzanne and John present."
— Joy Pullmann, Research Fellow at the Heartland Institute and Author of *The Education Invasion*

"In her excellent new book, written with John M. Townsend, Ph.D., an expert on the evolutionary roots of sex differences, Suzanne helps women see nature's truths. In doing so, she provides a roadmap for what most women want most of all: a lifelong love with a special man."
— Steven E. Rhoads, Ph.D., Professor Emeritus, U. of Virginia, and author of *Taking Sex Differences Seriously*

WOMEN WHO WIN
at*Love*

How to Build a Relationship That Lasts

Suzanne Venker
John M. Townsend, Ph.D.

Post Hill
PRESS

A POST HILL PRESS BOOK
ISBN: 978-1-64293-104-4
ISBN (eBook): 978-1-64293-105-1

Women Who Win at Love:
How to Build a Relationship That Lasts
© 2019 by Suzanne Venker and John M. Townsend, Ph.D.
All Rights Reserved

Post Hill Press
New York • Nashville
posthillpress.com

Published in the United States of America

"How bizarre it is to have to argue the obvious, to have to prove over and over again what is self-evident. So let me be as offensive as I possibly can: men are men, and women are women."

—Mallory Millett

"The doctrine that sex differences are only socially constructed is wrong. Get it? Wrong."

—Jordan Peterson

"I'm in despair at how the people around me are currently treating even the discussion of the science of gender difference as taboo, 'alt-right,' or somehow evil. It's disorientating and quite scary. You see how ideology trumps reason in even the most intelligent of people."

—Will Storr

TABLE OF CONTENTS

A NOTE FROM SUZANNE

I have a nineteen-year-old daughter in college who, like most young women her age, enjoys an abundance of support and guidance with respect to her professional endeavors—as she should. What she will not receive is any encouragement or direction for what will someday collide with those professional endeavors and, more importantly, what will have *the single greatest effect on her happiness and well-being.*

Marriage and family.

The assumption is that women can, and should, map out their lives the way men map out theirs—as though the sexes are exactly the same. In the age of equality, we pretend. We pretend that women don't care about love and commitment, that they can move in and out of meaningless sexual relationships with no repercussions at all. We pretend that women don't want to get married, even though the reality show *Say Yes to the Dress* has been a runaway success for twelve years. And we pretend that a woman's response to having a baby won't be fierce and intense, and unique to her as a woman. We pretend all of this, even though the truth—that women are gloriously and demonstrably different from men, sexually and otherwise—is glaringly obvious to anyone who pays attention.

Those of us who are parents of both boys and girls become privy to these sex differences early on, when our daughters insist on being princesses and our sons turn every inanimate object they can into a gun—with zero direction from Mom and Dad.

But no one ever talks about it. Even at this stage of development, we don't acknowledge the role biology plays in our lives because admitting its impact is verboten. Boys and girls, and men and women, are supposed to be "equal," as in *the same*. What one sex can do the other can, too.

And that is very often true.

But it doesn't mean they want to.

Despite their many equal capabilities, men and women have wildly different needs and desires—yet this truth is ignored by those with a political agenda. The sham starts in childhood and continues into adulthood, aided in no small part by the birth control pill. Because, when we remove reproduction from the equation, men and women *do* lead strikingly similar lives. Both sexes get an education and move into the workplace. Both sexes live on their own (or with each other) and postpone marriage long as possible.

But then something happens. Somewhere around the age of thirty, most women—not men, *women*—have an epiphany. It is then when women realize their ability to conceive is waning, and they subsequently become consumed with thoughts of marriage and babies. Their careers firmly established, these women begin to wonder where and how family will fit in to their lives.

This same sense of urgency will not be felt by men, for the obvious reason: it is women, not men, who get pregnant. Men can wait as long as they want to form families, but women cannot. It is then when the light bulb goes off.

Perhaps the sexes aren't equal after all.

To wit, over Thanksgiving last year I had a lengthy conversation with a thirty-two-year-old newly married woman. She and her husband had been together for many years prior to the wedding, each pursuing their respective careers in several different cities. In the course of our conversation, Katy relayed her ambivalence about motherhood. She was angst-ridden about how children would fit in to the adult urban lives she and her husband had created and was despondent over the fact that her husband didn't seem to be fretting over this dilemma. "He's too relaxed about it all," she said.

It wasn't fair, she added, that he didn't feel as torn as she did about when to have kids and how to structure their lives to accommodate them. "He should!" she said. "We should be the same!" When I asked why she assumed her husband should be as anguished as she was, I learned that Katy was a feminist. "Our sexist society expects women to carry the burden," she said. "But work-family conflict should be shared equally."

It's not society's fault, I told her. Men and women are simply different. They don't come to the marriage table with the same set of emotional needs, desires, and expectations. They don't approach work-family conflict in the same way, and they don't respond to becoming fathers the same way that women respond to becoming mothers.

Like so many women her age, Katy believes men and women are "equal" as in *the same*. She's in the dark about the biological differences between the sexes. She's been conditioned to believe a lie.

∞

When we started this book, the plan was simple: to offer real life, data-driven advice about men, women, sex, and love that's grounded in common sense and devoid of gender propaganda. But I underestimated the challenges faced by Katy's demographic: millennials, or those who are now in their twenties and thirties.

Millennials are struggling in a unique way—for several reasons. One, many have fallen hook, line, and sinker for the popular narrative that women are oppressed by the "patriarchy"—and that, to rectify this supposed problem, the sexes must strive for equality, which in effect means sameness or interchangeability. What an exercise in futility!

Two, millennials are the generation most affected by divorce and as a result have few role models for lasting love. Three, they've been raised to believe they "deserve" the best and thus have unrealistic expectations of marriage. Four, they came of age in a world of smart-phones and social media, which has stunted their ability to form meaningful attachments with the opposite sex.

But **the single greatest problem millennial women face is that they've been groomed by the culture, as well**

as by their parents, to put marriage and family on the backburner and to instead focus exclusively on careers. This still-very-new way of moving through one's twenties and even early thirties has resulted in, among other things, a generation of self-supporting women who don't "need" husbands at all. It also encouraged women to treat relationships casually, as if moving in and out of countless sexual unions, or even living with men, is no big deal.

To put it another way: it upended marriage and dating as we knew it.

Today, the complementary relationship between the sexes is gone—as are clear, definable sex roles. Men and women no longer know who's supposed to do what: Who makes the first move? Who pays for dinner? Should a man still open the door for a woman? Who will stay home with the kids? Whose career will take precedence? These are the conflicts of modern love our mothers and grandmothers never had to face. And they're huge.

Women have also priced themselves out of the dating market. Take Laura, a thirty-four-year old successful lawyer (who was married once before in her twenties with no kids) who's frustrated because she can't find a husband. By focusing exclusively on her career, Laura's choices have dwindled considerably. The men she'd like to date are either already married or are interested in younger women. She gets the leftovers.

Or here's another example. Not long ago I received an email from a divorced real estate agent in Beverly Hills of all places who had this to say about her daughter:

Dear Suzanne,

    I just read about you, and I'd like to talk to you about my daughter who's a high achiever. She's a thirty-eight-year-old, well-educated (two Ivy League schools), creative, intelligent, sophisticated, loving, successful, attractive, with a model-like body, and surprisingly can't find a desired partner. I must say she wasted many years on several senseless relationships. She is now extremely unhappy that she doesn't have a partner and, most importantly, she wants to have children. She has consulted with a few relationship coaches, but she is still single. All of her friends are married with kids. I'm clueless why she can't find her desired partner. Thank you in advance for your help.

What no one told women like Laura and my emailer's daughter is that men and women are different when it comes to what they look for in a relationship (as well as how they think and behave while in that relationship). Most men, for instance, aren't overly concerned with a woman's educational and professional achievements. It's fine if you have them, but it's not a selling point.

Women, on the other hand, are very much concerned with a man's education and career goals—despite being economically independent themselves. That's called hypergyny: no matter how educated and/or wealthy a woman may be, she wants to be married to a man of equal or higher status.

There are two reasons hypergyny still reigns despite the so-called rise of women. One, most women want the option to leave the workforce for a specified period of time when they become mothers and will thus need a competent working husband in order to do so. Two, from a sexual standpoint, women are simply more attracted to dominant men. Not domineering—dominant. (Those are often conflated, but they are not the same thing.) They want a man who can take the lead when necessary.

Naturally, **this poses a problem for modern women, who now get the majority of college degrees, and, in some milieus, even out-earn men. We cheer this phenomenon as a victory for women, but is it? And if it is, why do we not concede its implications?** Because if women are becoming the dominant sex, and most women want to marry dominant men—well, now what?

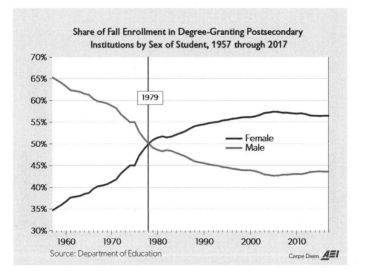

Share of Fall Enrollment in Degree-Granting Postsecondary Institutions by Sex of Student, 1957 through 2017

Source: Department of Education

Carpe Diem AEI

Of course, millennials aren't the only generation struggling in love. Plenty of women younger than twenty-five and over forty struggle, too. Many are divorced and still looking for love, while others are unhappily married. For this reason, we've divided the book into two sections: how to find love and how to sustain it. Either way, the message is the same.

You're struggling in love because of the way you think. Or rather, because of the way you've been taught to think. Change your mindset and you will get a different result.

Men are men, and women are women. They are not "equal." **The concept of sexual equality destroys love by denying the respective natures of women and men**. If you chuck the concept of gender equality and embrace the way men and women are made, your chances of building a relationship that lasts skyrocket. And isn't that the goal?

If so, let's do it!

Suzanne Venker
February 2019

Note: Throughout the book, it will sometimes be necessary for John or me to speak to the reader separately. We will make that note using either "SV" or "JMT."

A NOTE FROM JOHN

As a young man, I experienced the consciousness of the '60s and '70s. At the time, I truly believed the sexes were going to become more alike as we sloughed off our confining, outmoded sex roles and became freer, more self-actualized human beings. Like many young men in that era, I thought sexual liberation would mean women would become more like men. And in many ways, they have. But what I've discovered in my thirty years as an anthropologist is that the ancient process of conflict and negotiation between the sexes hasn't changed at all. Only the rhetoric has changed.

The freedoms conferred by effective contraceptives and women's economic independence have made men and women similar in some ways. But the cruel irony is that they've also allowed sex differences to become *more*, not less, pronounced.

When I was doing the research for my book, *What Women Want—What Men Want*, I encountered a great deal of resistance to my approach. It was strongest among academics and intellectuals who had absorbed the idea that sex differences were purely a product of socialization—a belief that is still with us today.

I understood the reasons for this resistance. First, many people misinterpret biosocial explanations. They assume such explanations are deterministic, that I'm saying human beings are like animals and are thus wired for certain behaviors that are immutable. Second, people still tend to think in terms of the nature-nurture dichotomy: a behavior is either caused by biology or by the environment. Third, people assume that biosocial arguments are fatalistic, cynical, or amoral. For instance, if I argue that men have a greater tendency than women to be physically violent or to be attracted to a variety of sexual partners, people think I'm saying it's acceptable for men to beat people up or cheat on their wives.

All of these assumptions are false. As human beings, we've inherited certain predispositions from our evolutionary past. Whether or not we choose to act on them is up to us. "Your biological nature sets the rules of the game, but within those rules you have a lot of leeway," notes clinical psychologist Jordan Peterson.[1]

Anyone who argues that we're born with no predispositions whatsoever, and that men and women would act exactly the same if society didn't teach them to act differently, is ignoring a mountain of evidence from the major scientific disciplines.

But that is precisely what ideologues do. They refuse to concede our biological tendencies—because if it's true they exist, then gender equality is unattainable. There's no hope for the brave new world feminists want to create.

Our answer to these questions is that knowledge is better than ignorance. Sex differences in sexuality and mate selection exist, and they are not going away. Information about these differences is therefore useful. This information enables people to make informed decisions about their relationships and offers a greater possibility of negotiating and reconciling these differences in their own lives.

The idea that sex differences are socially constructed may be the politically correct view, but it is based on ideology and wishful thinking rather than on empirical evidence. Biological and cross-cultural studies show — very clearly — that biology matters.

John M. Townsend, Ph.D.
February 2019

Please note that some of the material herein draws on John M. Townsend's previous work as a researcher on the evolutionary roots of sex differences.

PART ONE

BEFORE "I DO"

LANDING A HUSBAND IS LIKE landing a job: you have to be good at what you do to get hired. But how can you be good at something with which you've been given no guidance and had such little practice? The only things you've been told to do when it comes to love are to postpone marriage as long as possible (while enjoying the supposed benefits of commitment-free sex) and to make your career the center of your life.

This message has had an enormous impact on how women today structure their lives. Alexandra Solomon, a psychologist who teaches a course at Northwestern University called Marriage 101, says her students have absorbed the idea that love is secondary to academic and professional success. **"Over and over," she writes, "my undergraduates tell me they try hard not to fall in love during college, imagining that would mess up their plans."**[2]

This new attitude women harbor—not just in college but throughout their twenties—is in large part why dating is dead, and why it was subsequently replaced with what we call the "hookup," a vague term that can mean anything from hanging out together to having sex.

After all, what other option does a grown woman who's been groomed to be career-focused rather than fami- ly-focused have than to be casual with her body and her heart? If her professional life is considered *the number one most important thing*, there's no reason to date. The whole purpose of dating is to determine whether or not the other person is a match. Why go through all the rigmarole if marriage isn't on your radar? Might as well hookup until you're ready to settle down.

If only it were that simple.

In 2017, a documentary entitled *The Dating Project* addressed this subject by interviewing five men and women: two college students, one twenty-something, one thirty-something, and one forty-something—none of whom had ever been married. What we learn in the film is how lonely and frustrating it is to be single today, whether you're in college or out in the real world.

What this demographic knows how to do best is have sex. What they cannot fathom is the art of courtship, or how to develop a meaningful relationship with the oppo- site sex that may or may not lead to marriage but at very least makes a person feel secure and loved. They just skip to the end and wonder why they're dissatisfied.

How can this behavior possibly lead to a meaningful relationship or even marriage? **Committed long-term relationships don't *start* with sex; they *end* with sex.** Moreover, it is emotionally devastating for most women to move in and out of countless sexual unions that have no end goal. No one wants to admit this because women are supposed to be "just like men." But they're not.

It is much more difficult for a woman than it is for a man to give of herself in this way. She's not *designed* for hookups! What do we think all those films and television programs are about where the man and the woman have sex and he doesn't call her the next day so she thinks he's an ass? If women were "just like men," this would never have been a theme in the first place.

There are countless young women (and men!) today, both on college campuses and in the workforce, who would like to go out on actual dates but who have no idea how to go about it. Women in particular love the idea of traditional dating, but they've been told they *shouldn't* love it because it might interrupt their career plans.

That's a terrible message to impart to young women! It's also counterproductive to a happy life. "**Relationships and marriage [are] probably one of the most important things you're going to do in your life, right? But people don't spend any time doing anything about it**," notes Chris Donahue, one of *The Dating Project*'s producers.[3]

Indeed they don't.

We think it's time to change that.

1.

STOP TRYING TO HAVE
SEX LIKE A MAN

IN HER BOOK *UNPROTECTED*, former campus psychiatrist Dr. Miriam Grossman introduces the reader to Olivia, a college student at UCLA who had been valedictorian of her high school senior class and was planning to go to medical school. After she arrived on campus, Olivia had a short-term relationship with a young man. When it ended, she had bouts of bingeing and vomiting and ended up at the campus health center, where she met Dr. Grossman.

It turns out Olivia had had her first sexual experience with the young man, and she told Dr. Grossman she couldn't stop thinking about him. She especially couldn't handle seeing him in class. "Why," Olivia asked her, "do they tell you how to protect your body from herpes and pregnancy, but they don't tell you what it does to your heart?"[4]

Kerry Cohen, author of the memoir *Loose Girl*, can relate. In her book, Cohen examines her promiscuous past, which included sleeping with almost forty boys and men. *Loose Girl* analyzes in great detail all of the emotions that accompanied Cohen's sexual experiences. She reviewed the reasons why she had sex, why she chose the boys and men she did, how she felt leading up to each encounter, how she felt afterwards, and what she expected to happen compared to what actually did happen. At the end of the day, what Cohen wanted was for guys to like her. "I let these men inside me, wanting to make me matter to them."[5]

It is difficult to imagine the young man Olivia slept with having bouts of bingeing and vomiting and winding up at the campus health center as a result of his time with Olivia, just as it's difficult to imagine a young man authoring a book like Cohen's. The average guy who engages in commitment-free sex doesn't ruminate over who he had sex with or why he did it—he knows why he did it. Nor will he typically have sex with a woman because he wants her to like him. Many men have sex for no other reason than it's available. "For a man, this might be a pleasant trip down memory lane, counting up one's conquests," wrote Cohen. "But for a girl, it's a whole other story."[6]

A whole other story indeed.

Many women have sex to feel attractive and desirable, to prove to themselves or to others that they can "get" a good-looking, high status guy. But they're not really "getting" him at all. Most men will respond to an attractive woman who broadcasts her availability. Ergo, the woman who "gets" this man into bed isn't doing anything special or profound. What she really wants is his love—that *would* be special and profound—but she's not going to get it by sleeping with him.

That women become easily attached after sex isn't just limited to college women. In one of the sexual assault claims against disgraced movie mogul Harvey Weinstein, lawyers unearthed emails between Weinstein and his accuser that confirmed the relationship was consensual. The most significant exchange was this one: "I love you, always do," the woman wrote after the alleged attack. "But I hate feeling like a booty call."[7] Her message was followed up with a smiling-face emoji.

The takeaway is clear: when it comes to uncommitted sex, women are playing a game they can't win. **Feeling "used," or like a "booty call," is the *most common experience* of women who engage in casual sex, or "hookups," whether they're teenagers or grown women.** That just isn't the case for most men.

"Whether we like it or not, sex is intrinsically biased against the woman," writes Jennifer Joyner in a powerful article entitled "I Thought Casual Sex Would Be Empowering, but It Was the Opposite." She adds, "Biological reality dictates that she carries the brunt of sexual risk while he wields the majority of the sexual power. Make their coital relations mutually selfish—that is, primarily about fleeting pleasures and not about caring for the person—and [the woman] always loses."[8]

The Perfect Storm

The precise moment in history when the relationship between the sexes took a nosedive is when women en masse began to have sex like a man—casually, with no strings attached—under the guise that this behavior is liberating.

The perfect storm for this still relatively new behavior was the sexual revolution, which proudly promoted commitment-free sex, and the FDA's approval of The Pill—both of which occurred in the 1960s. Prior to that time, there was both a spoken and an unspoken narrative about sex: that it is meant for marriage—or, at the very least, for a committed adult relationship. It's true that people didn't always agree on the marriage point, but they did agree commitment was crucial.

But we overlooked something in our desire for commitment-free sex. Contraception may be useful for preventing pregnancy, but it can't do a thing about male and female nature. It can't make men and women sexual equals. Yet we operate under the delusion that it does. From college campuses to our nation's boardrooms, [many] women try to pursue sex the way men often do: no commitment necessary.

And they're getting burned.

In a qualitative exploration of college hookups, the authors of the journal article "The Casualties of Casual Sex," concluded (among other things) that women's response to casual sex is very different from men's:

> *The dominant notion of regret for females centered around shame and self-blame for engaging in sexual behaviors in the context of a hookup. Not knowing their partner and*

the lack of further contact with the partner seemed to compound their regrets and anger at themselves. The dominant notion of regret for males centered on disappointment over a bad choice of hookup partner. One female participant expressed this view: "During a hookup, females feel special, desirable, pretty; men feel hot and in control. Afterwards, females wonder if he's going to call, what it means, did she do the right thing. Males feel nothing. Males don't care, just as long as they get laid."[9]

In other words, many women today learn the hard way what their mothers or grandmothers have always known: sex for women is not the same as sex for men. **Most men can have sex with a woman to whom they are not emotionally attached and not lose sleep over it. That is not the case for most women.** Even the most sexually liberal woman is surprised to learn she cannot detach the way men can. She might appear to be indifferent in some encounters, but her reaction will often surprise her.

Take Alissa, twenty, who has had six one-night stands and, within the past year, two different sex partners. When asked whether she thought she should be emotionally involved with someone before having sex with a guy, her contradictory views speak volumes:

No, sex is not that big of a deal. When you first have sex, it is a big deal, but once you've lost your virginity, it gradually becomes less important to be in love with the guy. The more you have sex, the less of a big deal it becomes...I get attached to guys I have sex with very easily because I'm very emotional; I think this is natural for all girls. If the guy is really a jerk, though, and I have nothing in common with him, then it's a lot easier not to get emotionally involved than if I like the guy. Once I sleep with a guy, I feel that there is a bond between the two of us because we've shared our bodies and left ourselves vulnerable to each other. I think of the guy as being mine in a way, even though I know we don't have a relationship.

Jessica, twenty-one, has had six different sex partners within the past year and characterizes herself as a strong feminist who "doesn't need men in any way." She said having a career was very important to her, and she did not want to marry until she was about thirty.

In speaking with Jessica, she gave the impression she found casual sex acceptable. But elsewhere in the interview, she admitted she didn't engage in casual sex often because she didn't want to get hurt. She also said she was frustrated that she "could not find a formal date" on campus. Although it bothered her that the men she's interested in weren't willing to date, Jessica ignored the discrepancy between her permissive attitudes and her desire for commitment. She also saw no link between her promiscuous behavior and the inevitable outcome.

When I first go to bed with a guy, I wonder whether sex was all he was after and how he'll treat me in the morning. If I like the guy, I worry about whether he cares about me; otherwise, I don't care what he thinks. I'm not especially bothered by a one-night stand. I think of it as opening up; if it's only for one night, that's okay…I have to have control of myself. I can't get so wrapped up in [my boyfriend] that I forget about myself. I have to maintain my own personality and ideas. I don't want to lose what's important to me.

Amanda, twenty, has had sixteen one-night stands and, within the past year, three different sex partners. When asked whether she thought she should be emotionally involved with someone before having sex with him, she said no. Her emotions, however, quashed her attitudes and led her to reject casual sex.

If I had sex with a guy and I didn't like him, then I just wouldn't go out with him again. I would date other people. If I like the guy, then I do wonder whether sex was all he was after and how he will treat me in the morning; and I do think about marriage and what my family would think of him, what he would be like as a husband. I was very promiscuous when I was in high school, but within the last six months I have become very picky about who I sleep with. It was time to settle down and start getting serious about finding a husband. [She hopes to be married by age twenty-six.] Everyone should have their fun for a while and go crazy once they're away from their parents; but after a while, it isn't fun anymore and you want to start getting serious with someone. [Why?] I didn't like waking up with strange guys in strange places; it bothered me sometimes. It made me feel sort of used.

Ingrid, twenty-four, is a medical student in her mid-twenties who once dated a fellow classmate. Several months into their relationship, the young man began to feel confined and complained to Ingrid that he wanted more time alone and to be with his friends. Soon their relationship began to deteriorate. Ingrid and the young man fought, and she told him that if he could not devote more time and energy to her, she wasn't sure she wanted to continue the relationship. His response was to suggest they take a break.

Ingrid thought she and the young man would eventually make up, but a few days later he told her it was over. He said he wanted to maintain a "special friendship" with Ingrid in which they would see each other occasionally and sleep together. But Ingrid wanted more than that.

Several weeks later, when Ingrid was feeling lonely, she called the young man. She began to think that if *he* could handle sex on a casual basis, she could, too. So, Ingrid went over to his apartment and slept with him. Here's what she had to say afterward:

> *I knew within twenty-four hours after I saw him that he's not in love with me. He didn't call the next day, and I finally called him that night. He was studying, and after we talked a bit, he said, "Well, I've got to get back to studying!" I felt used, even though I don't think I should. It's irrational. If we had just gone out to dinner and talked, I would have felt he was interested in me. Or if he had called the next day, I wouldn't have felt bad. Instead I called him and went over and slept with him, and he got what he wanted. But I didn't. He says he wants a friendship, but I think he just wants to keep things friendly so it won't be uncomfortable in classes and then just sleep with me occasionally. That really bothers me. That's not even enough for a friendship. I thought I could handle it the way he does, but I couldn't and I feel pretty bad now about going over there.*

The common thread in all of these stories is that the women were often unable to separate sex and emotion. That whole "love 'em and leave 'em" thing just isn't a female practice — that's a guy thing.

Until recently, people understood and accepted this major difference between the sexes. They didn't know *why* men and women were different because the science wasn't there yet, but they knew it just the same. They knew it from experience, and they knew it in their gut.

Today we have proof. The female body, it turns out, is steeped in oxytocin and estrogen, two chemicals that together produce an environment ripe for attachment. Oxytocin, known primarily as the female reproductive hormone, is particularly relevant. Oxytocin causes a woman to bond with the person with whom she's intimately engaged. It also acts as a gauge to help her determine whether or not she should trust the person she's with.

Men have oxytocin, too, but a smaller amount. They're more favored with testosterone—which controls lust, not attachment. That's why *women*, not men, wait for a text the next day after a one-night stand. When a woman has sexual contact of any kind, it's an emotional experience, whether she intends it to be or not. The moment touch occurs, oxytocin gets released and the attachment process begins. It just doesn't happen the same way for men.

As a result of these circumstances, there does exist a double standard in which men can "get away with" having casual sex in a way women cannot. But this double standard doesn't *cause* men and women to behave differently, as we often hear from the culture. It exists *as a result of* men's ability to separate sex and emotion. That's not to say men *should* sleep around simply because they can. It just means it's common knowledge that they have less to lose. That's the underlying reason for the double standard.

It is true more women than ever are engaging in premarital sex, often without a great deal of courtship beforehand. But this behavior does not in any way alter the unique sexual psychologies of women and men. In other words, **women can try and *act* like men all they want. But the results will be drastically different.**

Sexual Arousal

In my class on human sexuality (JMT), a student mentioned that a female professor told her students it was a tragedy that sexist roles in our society make men think they have to get an erection every time they see an attractive woman. I asked my students what they thought of this statement, and one of my male students said the following:

> *There is no thinking involved. You see a good-looking woman with a great body, and you want to have sex with her. It's instantaneous. There's no decision. Of course, you can suppress it, but the initial thought is there.*

This young man's statement launched a class discussion about sexual arousal, whereupon we reviewed together the most recent studies. The research indicated that high school boys and college-age men are aroused two or three times a day on average, and that the stimulus for arousal is usually visual. In contrast, the average high school girl or college woman is aroused once or twice per *week*, and the stimulus for arousal is almost never the mere sight of a person or an object.

The college men agreed some erections are even spontaneous and involuntary and could occur in embarrassing situations, such as the classroom or even church. Merely *looking* at a girl across the room or allowing one's thoughts to stray to sexual images could produce arousal, and the sexual urge could be so strong that a man would seek relief by masturbating in a bathroom stall or some other desperate location.

> The sexual urge could be so strong that a man would seek relief by masturbating in a bathroom stall or some other desperate location.

The women in my class were incredulous and admitted this must be "awful." They wondered how boys and men could live like this, at which point a basketball player in my class smiled and explained that spontaneous, involuntary arousal was most common in puberty, and that "with experience you learn to control it" so that by eighteen or so men only experience erections when they allow them.

This type of visual sexual arousal doesn't exist for women. Women can be excited about seeing a handsome stranger on the street, or even about the possibility of meeting him, but they're not typically aroused sexually. For women, that requires touch.

The evolutionary explanation for a woman's more conservative arousal mechanism is both obvious and plausible: women get pregnant, and men do not. If women could be aroused by visual stimuli, they'd be taking part in hundreds of undesirable unions!

Men's motives for engaging in casual sex, as well as their emotional reactions to it, are different from women's. For men, merely having sex with someone, even with partners they did not like, was pleasurable—or at least pleasurable enough to continue doing it.

Matt was twenty-one years old and had had sixteen one-night stands. With fifteen of his partners, he knew before he had sex with them that he did not want to get emotionally involved. When asked why he went ahead and had sex in those circumstances, he said the following:

> *To get laid. I did this about twice a week. I'd see them at a bar and take them home. This was enough because I was not attracted to them. I wasn't willing to take these girls out on a real date. I'd see them in a bar and start talking a little and chat more and more as the evening progressed, and then we'd go to my place. I got sick of these girls after a while. I was kind of seeing this girl for a while who was too nice, like she was too materialistic and tried too hard*

to make the relationship work. She was looking for a husband. She would never stand up to me. It was really a turn off. [Did you still have sex with her?] Oh, I still screwed her for a long time, even though I didn't like her.

Mark, also twenty-one, did not think sex without love was okay. He felt he should be emotionally involved with a person before having sex and said he thought about marriage and the long-term possibilities of a relationship when he had sex with someone. He said he respected women and that "before we become lovers, we must be friends. We are equals."

In many of his statements, Mark appeared to reject typical male attitudes toward sex and showed the kind of sensitivity many women say they prefer. Nevertheless, Mark had had six one-night stands, and, within the past year, three sex partners. With six of the women, he knew before he had sex with them that he did not want to get emotionally involved. When we asked why he had sex with them, he replied:

They were available. If a girl wants to put out, I won't turn her down. As soon as you get your fraternity pin, a whole group of women becomes available to you that otherwise wouldn't give you the time of day. Now I get approached a lot at parties and in bars. I don't know why, maybe it's my haircut. I don't think

I'm "alternative," but I do make my own style. I think girls see me as the house rebel. That's my rep, you know, like a James Dean. That's why they come on to me. I usually prefer to date girls that are younger than me because they're easier to screw.

Some of the young men I interviewed felt guilt over their activities and thus reduced their number of partners from what it would have otherwise been. But this guilt was inspired by their partners' *reactions to casual relations rather than by their own reactions: really hurting a woman by "just screwing and dumping her" made some of the men "feel like shit."*

Rob is a senior and in a fraternity. He explained his feelings as follows:

I had sex with girls I didn't like because it was convenient. They were really into me, and it made me feel really guilty, which is why it was hard to stay detached emotionally. We'd have sex a couple of times a week. I would have preferred less, but they were wanting it more, thinking it was what I wanted. The whole thing didn't feel right. If a woman wanted just sex, it would be cool; but they always get involved. That's why I usually only sleep with girls I really like. I really hate hurting girls. It makes me feel guilty.

Rob's observation—"If a woman wanted just sex, it would be cool; but they always get involved"—proved to be true when I spoke to women who *thought* they could "act like a man" but whose interviews proved otherwise. Despite the women being sexually liberal, there were feelings of being more vulnerable than men after intercourse; and they were more interested in the long-term possibilities of a relationship and found it difficult to keep from getting emotionally involved. For this reason, the women wouldn't continue to have sex with a guy they didn't like if they saw it wasn't going to lead to something more permanent.

Now perhaps you're a woman who insists she can handle commitment-free sex. "I'm not looking to get married right now," you say, "so it's fine." And you may not, in fact, be looking to get married. But we don't believe for a moment that you don't want *something* to come from a hookup. Almost every woman wants a relationship of some sort, even if she's not ready to marry. **No matter what stage of life she is in, it is a rare woman who just wants sex.** On the contrary, a woman's enjoyment of sex depends on whether or not she has a committed relationship with a man she can trust—and this takes time to build.

#Metoo

That most men can separate sex and emotion more easily than most women can isn't the end of the conversation. There's also this: a "booty call," or a random hookup, does not lead to the kind of relationship most women crave. Nothing proves this to be true better than the #Metoo movement.

After the deserved fall of a few very powerful men, stories of supposed sexual harassment that turned out to be nothing more than a date gone bad—the most infamous being the one between Aziz Ansari and Katie Way, who accused Ansari of sexual coercion in an article for the website *Babe*—began to surface. These stories demonstrate how vastly different men and women approach uncommitted sex.

In fact, it was #Metoo that led *The New York Times* to hire Jessica Bennett, former columnist at *TIME* and author of the book *Feminist Fight Club*, as its new "gender editor." Her first article? "When Saying 'Yes' Is Easier Than Saying 'No.'"

In the article, Bennett blames "dangerously outdated gender norms" for causing her and her contemporaries to feel awkward and embarrassed when they engage in casual sex, the implication being that if society didn't *expect* women to behave in a certain way, they'd be able to have sex like a man.

What an absurd spin on reality! It's *contemporary* gender norms, not traditional gender norms, that have landed women in this uncomfortable place. It is impossible to imagine any woman prior to, say, 1990, claiming it's "easier" to have sex with a man than it is to say no to him. Yes, there have always been men who don't like to take no for answer; but it was still the norm for women to say it and to subsequently be heard and respected.

"Traditional mores set the default for premarital sex at 'no,' at least for females," writes Heather Mac Donald. "This default recognized the different sexual drives of males and females and the difficulties of bargaining with the male libido. The default 'no' to premarital sex meant that a female did not have to negotiate the refusal with every opportuning male; it was simply assumed. She could, of course, cast aside the default assumption; that was her power and prerogative. But she did not have to provide reasons for shutting down a sexual advance."[10]

Indeed, Bennett's premise that it's "easier" to say yes than it is to say no to a guy proves sexual equality is a fraud. After all, if it were true that women are "just like men" in their ability to disentangle sex and emotion, why would women be so quick to cry foul after a botched sexual encounter? Why would office sex become a cause for the courts rather than a welcome ride? (Pun intended.)

> The female sex drive is not equal to the male sex drive. It can't be, otherwise we'd all be humping each other like rabbits.

The excesses of #Metoo speak volumes about women's *weakness*, not their strength, in the aftermath of the perfect storm. The sexual revolution and The Pill didn't empower women. It *dis*empowered them by removing a woman's ability to say no and have that be the end of it.

We as a nation have sanctioned commitment-free sex (with no complaints from men, thank you very much), and what do we have to show for it? What have we learned? That the female sex drive is *not* equal to the male sex drive. It can't be, otherwise we'd all be humping each other like rabbits, and marriage and families would never be formed.

There's a reason, in other words, that men and women aren't the same sexually. The fact that women have babies and men do not is not some trivial matter—it's the whole enchilada. <u>Birth control doesn't change a woman in the least; it simply gives the illusion she's just like a man. But she's not.</u>

A woman's need to bond with a man, to feel safe and loved and committed to, is critical for her to feel happy, healthy, and whole. It also channels male lust into something meaningful. That women think beyond the physical, that they enter into emotional territory quickly as a result of sex, is something to celebrate, not something to denigrate or eradicate.

Just imagine if every parent taught their daughters and sons to embrace it.

●●●

Principle 1

Your body isn't built for casual sex.
●●●

2. MASTER THESE 8 DATING RULES

IN THE 1950s, that oft-ridiculed era when women all over the country were purportedly miserable, marriage proposals were so common women had to turn down several potential husbands before deciding on the right one.

That was certainly the case for my mother (SV), who was born in 1930. As a young girl, I would find countless love letters from Charlie, George, Frank—and others whose names I can't recall—that all contained marriage proposals. They were stored in my mother's memory box, and I would sift through them and marvel at what it was like to have so many men pining for you.

Justice Sandra Day O'Connor, also born in 1930, is another example of the times. Prior to becoming engaged to her husband, O'Connor turned down several marriage proposals, including, ironically, one from fellow Supreme Court Justice William Rehnquist, her then-law school classmate. "Dating was pretty innocent in the '50s,"[11] O'Connor's son Jay told NPR.

Innocent, yes—and for good reason: dating was serious business. Since marriage was the goal, dating was viewed as a precursor to the rest of people's lives, and was thus given the weight it deserves. It was also understood that the more time men and women spent together, or the longer they dated, the more likely the relationship would become physical. That, combined with a lack of reliable birth control, forced couples to keep things light.

One advantage of this approach is that it allowed men and women to easily "date around," or to go out alone with different members of the opposite sex and get to know them well—minus the sex. Not only did this allow for objectivity, it makes sense that under these circumstances a woman might get more than one proposal.

Of course, a lot has changed since the 1950s, the most significant difference being the "perfect storm" we wrote about in chapter one. The combination of the birth control pill and the sexual revolution, when women were encouraged to have sex like a man, permanently altered the male-female dynamic. As a result, marriage proposals vanished. Why buy the cow when you can get the milk for free?

To be fair, it isn't just men who are postponing marriage. Women are, too. There are some men today who'd be happy to marry their girlfriends, but the women keep putting it off because they're uber-focused on their careers. They're also waiting for that "perfect" guy. We know of many stories in which women passed over a guy they know would have made a great husband because they believed they could do better. This is a mistake. While these women are looking around for that "perfect" guy (who, for the record, doesn't exist), their age impairs their chances for marriage much more so than it does for men.

As we mentioned earlier, somewhere around the age of thirty, these same women will start to panic as they become aware of their declining fertility. This is the modern generation's first awakening that sex differences are real. And from that point on they only magnify.

The number-one reason thirty-something women have trouble finding husbands is that they simply waited too long—by that time the pool of marriageable men has dwindled. Men can afford to wait, but women must be more strategic. We won't argue that it's unfair, but none of us can do anything about it.

Now you might say in response, "Well, even if I reject the premise of the sexual revolution, it's not like we can go back to the way things were prior to The Pill!"

To which we'd say: Why not? Pill or no pill, women can choose to close their legs—or to say "no" to casual sex—anytime they want. If enough women do, the tide will eventually turn. A man can't have access to a woman without her permission—that's called rape. And contrary to what we hear in the media, most men aren't rapists.

And even if the tide doesn't turn, there's no reason for *you* to go down with the ship. Don't worry about what others are doing. If marriage is the goal, below are eight dating rules to help guide you on your journey.

The 8 Dating Rules

Rule #1 Let him chase you.

There's a cardinal rule in dating that, until recently, has been known and accepted by just about everyone: the man does the pursuing. <u>The natural order of things is for the man, not the woman, to take the lead.</u> After all, you want to be the woman he desperately wants out of all the other women he could have, don't you? Well, there's only one way to do that.

Let him come to you.

You need to be the woman who doesn't act all googly-eyed around the guy you like, even if your heart goes pitter patter when you're near him. Don't let him know how you feel! Play it cool. Let him think you're too wrapped up in your own happy life to give him the time of day. Men love a challenge and are competitive by nature. They pride themselves on getting the girl other men would love to have.

> When a man is interested in you, *you will know it*. There will be zero confusion on your part. Zero. Nada.

If you reverse this dynamic by being the one who makes the overture, you may indeed get a positive response. However, you will never know if the guy is just being polite or if he's actually "into" you. Because when a man is interested in you, *you will know it*. There will be zero confusion on your part. Zero. Nada. None.

Men go after what they want, and you will want him to go after you because if he doesn't, not only will you never know his true intentions, he won't be the assertive man you'll need him to be down the road. There will be countless times in your life when you will want your man to stand up for himself, and for you, and for your possible children. And if the guy you like lacks the assertiveness to ask you out, he will likely disappoint you down the line.

We know this sounds blasphemous since women today are taught to be "go-getters." However, as I (SV) wrote about in my last book, *The Alpha Female's Guide to Men & Marriage*, you can't behave the same way in love as you do at work. Those are two entirely separate domains. Being aggressive at work is fine; being aggressive in love is not. That's his job.

I was very fortunate to have been raised by parents who hailed from the Greatest Generation and were thus not prone [to] political correctness. My mother taught me the kinds of things the women of her generation taught *their* daughters. "Let the guy come to you," she'd say. "Men don't respect what they don't have to work for, so play hard to get." This would ultimately be followed up with instructions to never call a boy and to not even *think* of asking him out!

Such advice may be old-school, but that doesn't mean it doesn't work—it just means it's old school. So what? The modern plan, where women actively pursue men and have sex with them before a relationship has even been established, is disastrous. One of my subjects (JMT), a female medical school student who'd slept with roughly twenty-five men, made the following observation: "If you have sex the first time you go out with a guy, you've given up the game point. There's nothing for him to work for."

The bottom line, in other words, is that if the guy you like isn't the one doing the chasing, if he doesn't think you're the best thing since sliced bread and doesn't move mountains to go out with you, he's not your man.

Also, keep in mind that many guys will respond to a woman's overture, especially if she's pretty, even if he's not necessarily "into" her. They may also keep a relationship going because they like the sex and don't want to hurt the woman's feelings by breaking it off, thus making her feel there's hope when there isn't any.

Conversely, when a guy *is* "into" you, *you will know it.* There will be no question in your mind as to how he feels, so you won't need to talk him in to anything! Don't waste years of your life with any guy who doesn't fit the bill. In other words, **don't be the man in the relationship**. Let him come to you.

Unfortunately, too many women don't put this dynamic to the test. Instead, they jump into the male role and then wonder why their relationships don't work out. To avoid this mess and confusion, reject the notion that it doesn't matter who makes the first move. It does matter. Just because you're capable of being the man in the relationship doesn't mean you *should* be the man. If the goal is marriage or even a long-term relationship, don't be the hunter.

Be the hunted.

Rule #2 Don't offer to pay.

There are three reasons why a woman shouldn't pay on a date. The first is, as per Rule #1, the man presumably asked *you* out—not the other way around. And the person who asks should be the person who pays.

Second, when a man pays, he's demonstrating to you that you're worth spending his hard-earned money on. Don't refuse his overture! Instead, learn to receive with graciousness. Just smile and say thank you. Being able to receive, as opposed to undermining a man's attempt at being chivalrous, is a crucial part of the dating process. A man will take his cues from you.

Third, accepting a man's willingness to pay says a lot about *you*. It lets him know that you value yourself, that you believe you're worth spending hard-earned money on. And that's a great place to start any relationship.

Offering to pay your half of the date cheapens the experience and makes it feel no different from two friends grabbing a bite. A date is different from hanging out with a friend—or at least, it's supposed to be. Just because you're capable of paying your way doesn't mean you should. Let him take care of it.

Rule #3 Never have more than two drinks.

If you look up the stats on alcohol consumption for Americans of all ages, it's an extremely high number. We get it, and we're not telling you to abstain from drinking altogether on your dates. We are, however, emphatically suggesting you never move beyond drink two.

What you do on your own time or with your girl-friends is one thing. But getting drunk on dates, or even on semi-dates (going out with another couple, going to a formal if you're in college) is the equivalent of shooting yourself in the foot. You might as well have not had the date at all if you're going to be drunk while you're on it.

How much you should drink will mean something different for everyone, depending on your weight and your tolerance. But a good rule of thumb is to never have more than two drinks. And if we're talking stiff martinis, drink it slowly and stop at one. Because here's what we know for sure: sex and alcohol are a potent mix. Nothing good can come of it, and much can be lost.

The purpose of a date is to get to know the other person, and you can't do that if you're drunk. We also want you to follow Rule #6, and #Rule 6 will likely be broken if you have that third drink. How many women do you know who hook up with guys while they're sober?

Exactly.

So be smart and stop at drink two.

Rule #4 Don't be the giddy girl in slutty clothes.

One of the things that's changed considerably over the years is the way women dress and behave in the company of men. There's an inherent respect that comes from dressing classy and from maintaining a certain decorum when you're out with a man. This has unfortunately been lost in an era of "anything goes."

What we wear says a lot about what we think of ourselves and how we want others to think of us. We get back what we put out into the world. Ergo, if you dress slutty, you'll attract a man who just wants to "get some" because that's the vibe he picks up from you. If you dress classy, you'll attract a man who wants to get to know *you*. We're not suggesting that you dress like a nun—it's fine to accentuate what you've got! Just do it in a classy—rather than in a slutty—fashion.

We know dresses aren't exactly in vogue, but just so you know: men *love* dresses. And you might like it too! When you wear a dress, you will immediately feel more feminine than when you wear, say, a pair of jeans. Women exude femininity when they wear a dress, and feminine energy is crucial for attracting a man. Just do an experiment one day: wear a dress and see if you notice the number of men who respond. It's pretty shocking.

The way you behave matters, too. If you're giggly and silly, that too is the caliber of man you'll attract: many men will choose to score with the flightiest girl in the room. If you talk in a more mature or serious manner, you'll attract

WOMEN WHO WIN AT LOVE

a man of substance. And we assume you want a man of substance.

So, don't let it all hang out when you're on a date. Don't talk to him the same way you talk with your girl-friends. Your date is not your girlfriend. In other words, don't be the fun, drunk party girl. A man will date—he'll certainly have sex with!—that girl, but he won't marry her. Party girls are the women guys date until they find the one who's marriage material.

Be *that* girl.

Rule #5 Don't tell the men you date how smart and successful you are.

We have some news that may come as a shock: men don't care how smart and successful you are. It's not that men aren't interested in what you do for a living—they are—but they will notice if what you do has taken over your life. That's not a selling point. So don't talk about how "busy" you are or about how you travel so much or about how your career is your life and your identity.

For one thing, your career *shouldn't* be your life and your identity. Moreover, when you go on and on about your career with a man you're dating, what do you think that tells him? It says, "I do not have time for you. There is something more important in my life, and you'll get the leftovers."

It's true you may go out of your way to give your guy more attention at the start of the relationship, but don't think for a moment he isn't thinking ahead. Men know women will do what it takes to reel a guy in. He'll notice what's important to you on the very first date; and if your career is all you talk about, that tells him all he needs to know.

Rule #6 Don't have sex with him on the first, second, or twentieth date.

We know it's hard to imagine a time when women didn't have sex before marriage, but the fact that women now have sex with men before *a relationship* has even been established speaks volumes. Yet sadly, that is where we are.

In a December 2018 cover story in *The Atlantic*, author Kate Julian reported that casual sex, or "hookups," are considered easier (of course we know from Chapter 1 this isn't the case for women) because people don't have to worry about getting attached. Forget premarital sex. Now "relationship sex," or sex within the context of an exclusive relationship in which an attachment has been formed, is officially passé.

Given these new attitudes, it will sound old-fashioned to suggest you not have sex with a guy until a relationship has been firmly established (which takes many months), but just because something's unpopular doesn't mean it's wrong. If the goal is lasting love, having sex with a guy before he's fallen for you will not get you where you want to go.

The truth is, if uncommitted sex were truly liberating you wouldn't be reading this book. Hooking up says more about you than it does anything else. To willingly let countless men have their way with you, or to have sex with one's friends, is in fact proclaiming how *little* you think of yourself. Either that or you're confused about the link between love and sex.

Sex with a guy won't bring you love. It doesn't work that way.

When it comes to sexuality, women have engaged in a gigantic social experiment—and the damage has been profound. Some learn the lesson about casual sex after a sordid night or two, while others don't begin to understand or even acknowledge the ramifications for years—sometimes when it's too late. What makes the message so insidious is that young women are prone to feeling insecure and are thus vulnerable to the idea that sleeping with a guy will make them more attractive.

It doesn't.

It makes you a cheap lay.

Have you seen *Pride and Prejudice*? If you haven't, you should. (*Sense & Sensibility* is another great example.) Even if you have, watch it again. Study the relationship between Elizabeth and Mr. Darcy, and you'll note the sexual energy that positively drips off the screen. (The same could be said about any classic film, really.) That's what happens when two people don't jump into bed together the moment they meet, or anytime soon afterward. A relationship develops, and the sex comes later. You can rarely reverse these two without it ending in heartache.

Rule #7 Give him space
(and live your own life in the meantime).

Speaking of *Pride & Prejudice*, if you've read it or watched it, you know that Wickham is the bad guy—a player, or a nineteenth-century "bad boy" (in *Sense & Sensibility*, the charming bad boy is Willoughby)—and Mr. Darcy is the good guy. He's rich and handsome, and very proud. Darcy has his pick of any woman he wants, but he's only interested in the woman who pays him the least amount of attention: Elizabeth.

Elizabeth doesn't throw herself at Darcy the way other women do, which makes him all the more interested in her. Elizabeth wants very much to get married, but she refuses to marry for money. She wants to marry for love, to a man of character—and it takes her a long time to figure out whether Darcy fits the bill. In the meantime, Elizabeth is patient and reserved and busies herself with her own life and interests. This makes Darcy fall in love with her even more.

When you live your own life and do your own thing, the man you like won't feel hemmed in and will be more interested in you as a result. Plus it tells him you're a fascinating woman who has interests and hobbies of her own, and he will want to know more about those things.

One of the reasons it's harder to get men to the altar is because they know that once they're there, they lose their freedom. Thus, the best thing you can do when you're dating is to not begrudge him his space. If he likes to go out with the guys, just say, "That's great! Have fun!" Don't ask yourself why he didn't ask you to come along or what it means that he didn't ask you to come along. Do not assume he doesn't like or love you as much as you like or love him.

Don't assume anything. Just give him space and find something else to do with your time.

Rule #8 Move on if he can't commit.

A great rule of thumb for deciding when it's time to jump ship is that if your guy hasn't proposed by the middle of year two, he's probably not going to. Naturally, this will be different if you're dating a guy at age twenty versus at age thirty. But if you *are* dating at age twenty, you're probably not planning to get married soon anyway.

Age has a lot to do with the question about how long you should stick with the same man. Most men won't commit in their early twenties because men mature later than women. That's why marriage-minded women have pretty much always dated older men.

Too many women waste years of their lives hoping they can talk a boyfriend (with whom they may or may not be living) into marriage or simply hope he'll change his mind about marrying them. Women who master the eight dating rules don't have to talk a man into anything— he'll be dying to marry you! Smart women also pick up on whether or not a man is marriage material early on (just as men do with women), and they don't stick around if he isn't. That's an exercise in futility.

You'll know when you're dating a man whether or not you and he are on the same page with respect to marriage. If you don't know, you're not communicating the way you should be. Either which way, the bottom line is this: **If your guy hasn't made any overtures, if you have to wonder what he thinks or, God forbid, have long discussions with him about the worthiness of marriage as an institution, run!** He is not the guy for you. Don't you want to marry a man who wants you so badly he can't wait to say "I do"?

Wait for *that* guy.

Are the rules different if I'm in college?

The eight dating rules are designed for any woman who's single, divorced or, yes, still in college. But you may need to tweak them a bit since marriage probably isn't on your radar. Even so, we know that *relationships* are on a college woman's mind (though she may pretend otherwise), and the rules above apply to committed relationships as much as they do to marriage.

In fact, a university campus is fertile ground for relationship exploration. The problem is that on campuses today, dating has taken a back seat to hookups. And while we know that doesn't necessarily mean intercourse, it's still about getting naked with a man you barely know.

This practice may be commonplace, but that doesn't mean it's harmless.

On the contrary, casual sex is a disaster. "People treat sex like it's casual. It's not," notes clinical psychologist Jordan Peterson. "Sex is unbelievably complicated. It's dangerous. It involves emotions. It involves pregnancy. It involves illness. It involves betrayal. It reaches right down into the roots of someone. You don't play with something like that casually. Well, you can, but you'll pay for it."[12]

And women pay the most. Not only are they the sex that gets pregnant and that's more likely to contract an STD, they're also the sex that gets easily attached. Most women don't even gain *sexually* from this type of encounter. It's very difficult for a woman to have an orgasm with a man she barely knows because to let go in that way requires vulnerability. And vulnerability requires trust. And trust takes time to build.

A man, on the other hand, doesn't need to trust a woman in order to have an orgasm. He can have one lickety-split! So at the end of the day, **it's not women but young men who gain the most from America's new sexual landscape**. We transitioned from married sex, to uncommitted sex, to hooking up—or to not being able to attach ourselves to anyone at all.

How on earth is this progress?

Take Cecilia from *The Dating Project*, the film we mentioned earlier. Cecilia hadn't had a date in years and tells a story about a recent date she had in which the man did nothing more than touch her arm. Cecilia had forgotten what it was like to have genuine physical contact with a man, so when he made this gesture she "wanted to cry." As Cecelia tells her story, she chokes up and asks the film crew to "cut" by waving her hand in front of the camera.

Welcome to the sad state of singlehood.

But how can I follow these rules, you wonder, if men on campus don't know how to ask a woman out on a date? What if all anyone knows is how to text? What if social media has changed everything, and we can never go back?

> If you want a real relationship rather than a roll in the hay, you have to stop rolling in the hay.

Believe it or not, this is fixable. **Relationship dynamics will change the moment women demand more from themselves and from men**. If women raise their standards by not taking part in the hookup culture and by not supplanting the male role, things will change. The actress Mae West once said, "When women go wrong, men go right after them." And women have gone wrong! Which means when they go right, men will have no choice but to respond.

Indeed, **women are the relationship navigators: men will respond to whatever women demand**. First it was marriage—and men came to the table. Then it was commitment-free sex—and men came to that table, too. If women change it back again, perhaps not to "no sex until marriage" but *at least* to "no sex until love," men will have no choice but to submit to those terms. And this, in turn, will lead to more meaningful relationships, many of which will transition to marriage.

To put it another way: You, as a woman, have all the power. If you want a real relationship rather than a roll in the hay, you have to stop rolling in the hay. Instead, implement these eight dating rules into your life. And watch what happens.

• •

PRINCIPLE 2

Women are the relationship navigators:
men will respond to whatever they demand.
• •

HOW *NOT* TO BE 30 WITH NO MAN AND NO PLAN

"...And the princess became CEO of a Fortune 500 company and lived happily ever after."

HOW DO WE put this gently?

You've been screwed.

That is to say, you've been woefully unprepared for the reality of what your future will most likely look like. A job, or career, is just one part of life—and not even the best part. The best part of life is finding someone to love who loves you back. Indeed, whom you choose to marry and the quality of that marriage will have more effect on your happiness and well-being than anything else in your life. Nothing even comes close.

Why, then, do we not prepare women for this critical juncture in their lives? **Why do we tell women like you to focus exclusively on work and to ignore the part about marriage and babies**? "There are a great many women unhappy because they acted upon the wisdom passed along to them by the people they most trusted," writes Danielle Crittenden in her aptly titled book, *What Our Mothers Didn't Tell Us.* "These women thought they did everything right—only to have it turn out all wrong. That the wisdom they received was faulty, that it was based on false assumptions, is a hard lesson for anyone to learn."[13]

Here's Kelsey's story.

> *I'm turning thirty in January 2019. With that thirty-year mark approaching, I've been going through a multitude of changes of heart and thought. In order to explain them, I need to reveal some context.*
>
> *From the ages of sixteen to twenty-four, I lived in New York City. In those years, I was surrounded by private school educators and adults who force-fed a distinctly feminist narrative that I didn't recognize as such at the time. It has only been in my own personal reflection that I'm beginning to see the impact of that*

message and have examined some of the choices I made along the way as a result—choices that have led me to my current predicament.

The reason I moved to New York originally was to pursue a career in the entertainment industry. From the time I was fifteen until about twenty-four, my number-one focus and desire was to become a famous recording artist and have a successful career in the industry. I found myself surrounded by young women that were on a similar path, albeit for different but equally difficult career choices.

We were all extremely focused on getting ahead and having high-profile careers. Never once did I consider marriage, family, or what I would do if my chosen career path did not work out according to my vision. I grew up in an environment where you were taught to never depend on a man, that marriages were likely to fail, and that having kids would destroy the prospect of a high-flying career. I did not want kids at the time and wasn't sold on being married at all.

I was starting to become disenchanted with the music business and moved away from New York at the end of 2014. I was burned out on the city and on the high cost of living. And quite frankly, I never felt that I totally fit in in New York.

Around the same time, I got involved in a serious relationship. I eventually moved in with my boyfriend, and we started a business together. We have been together three and a half years and have spent loads of time with each other's families and have completely intertwined our lives with a home, business, etc.

When I turned twenty-nine, I started to have the very normal feelings of wanting to get married and potentially have a family. But here's the problem: we never discussed our viewpoints on marriage, kids, or otherwise early on in our relationship. I just assumed because I felt a certain way at twenty-five that I would feel that way at thirty.

Well, I am here to say that that is not at all true. *Today, my boyfriend and I are not on the same page at all when it comes to these very important factors for planning a future. "Playing house" has been fun and much easier to maintain financially; but by doing so, I don't believe my boyfriend is in any hurry to propose.*

I take care of about 75 percent of the household work on top of running my own small marketing business and mutually working our shared business interests in music. By living together, I've completely destroyed the incentive for him to make a commitment. Why would he want to marry when I'm already a "wife"?

He also "isn't sure" he wants to have a family, which of course leaves me in limbo.

I still sing in a band full time in the project he and I work in together, but I'm getting worn out by the unpredictable nature of playing music for a living—specifically, the late nights and unhealthy environment of the bar scene. I'm not sure what I want to do yet; but I know that I want a multi-faceted life, with time for family, work, friends, keeping myself in shape/ healthy, traveling, and having a home.

I have many interests, none of which I've set myself up well for pursuing. If I want a family, it is unlikely that two freelance musicians—even if my boyfriend wanted to get married—would be able to support that goal. I'm feeling pressure of a ticking clock and having to make some tough decisions.

My boyfriend wants to pursue his music career, and I support him in that fully; but his goals do not align with mine. It sucks and it's hard. The thought of going back into the dating scene makes me nauseous, especially as the dating pool dwindles and my friends are settling down with weddings and new homes. I feel totally stuck, unprepared, and unsure of what to do.

I know because of the narrative millennial women have been conditioned to believe, via

> *movies, television, and even by our own parents*
> *that I can't be alone in this struggle. If I could*
> *go back in time, I would have pursued the*
> *same things; but I would have accepted the fact*
> *earlier on that I should also plan accordingly*
> *for the other things that make a well-rounded*
> *life—including marriage, family, career, and a*
> *partner who's on the same page.*

How can you avoid landing in Kelsey's boat? Reject the messages you receive from the culture (and possibly from your parents) about how to structure your life. Instead, think long term and plan accordingly. You need to be as intentional about your personal life as you are about your professional life. More, actually.

Your career path will ebb and flow, possibly even recede. But **whom you choose to marry, and how that marriage fares, will be the axis upon which all other decisions are made.** If you get it wrong, you can't just undo it and start over. Well, you can try, but the divorce rate for second marriages hovers around 70 percent, so we don't recommend it.

Countless women have learned this lesson the hard way simply because they were taught to focus solely on their career, as if work should be their raison d'être and the rest of life should orbit around it. That's a terrible plan. As a woman, you're going to respond to marriage and children differently than men will, which means you must map out your future in a way that takes this into account.

In a December 2018 cover story for *The Atlantic*, author Kate Julian writes about what the magazine dubs a "sex recession," or the trend of young people—women *and* men, apparently—putting sex and relationships on the back burner. In Julian's attempt to understand the reasons behind it, one young man she interviewed told her there's tremendous pressure from parents and other authority figures "to focus on the self, at the expense of relationships"—pressure, Julian adds, that twenty-somethings have told her extends "right on through college."[14]

Another young woman told Julian that when she was in high school, her parents, who are both professionals with advanced degrees, had discouraged relationships on the grounds that they might diminish her focus. Even today, in graduate school, this young woman finds the attitude hard to shake. "Now I need to finish school, I need to get a practice going, I need to do this and this, and then I'll think about love. But by thirty, you're like, 'What is love? What's it like to be in love?'"[15]

Karla, a second-year medical student I (JMT) interviewed, is another example.

> *I'll be twenty-five when I graduate, and thirty by the time I get going. I'll have to ask how fertile I am and how many opportunities I'll have to meet men. Thirty is a milestone. You only have five years left to have kids before you take serious genetic risks. Men have the advantage; they don't even have to think of this. A lot*

of these men will be in their residencies before they even think of marriage. They can afford to fool around. I can't afford to spend a year in a relationship with a man I don't intend to marry. I don't have the time.

Karla is right: women don't have time. According to clinical psychologist Meg Jay, 80 percent of life's most defining moments take place by age thirty-five. That's why **the best time to make important decisions about your personal life is in your twenties, not in your thirties.** If you don't have every detail laid out (who does?), that's okay. You still need to have a general idea of what you want, and you still need to know a few things in advance so you can factor them into your plans.

Here are three:

1. **What's important to you now will not be important to you later.** At twenty, your career will feel like the most important thing in life. At thirty, you'll likely have babies on your mind. And once you have those babies, mark my (SV) words: you will change. Dramatically. In fact, you may not even recall the person you were before you became a mother. And that's okay—because who you turn out to be as a result of becoming a mother is far better than who you were before.

2. **Your body has a clock, and your boyfriend's does not.** Men can postpone marriage longer

than you can because they can always move on if the relationship ends and have children with a younger woman. You don't have this luxury. Women are far more fertile between twenty-eight and thirty-five than they are after thirty-five. This topic has become political, but it shouldn't be. It just is what it is.

3. **You will very likely want to take care of your babies and will thus need a man on whom you can rely, if only for a few years.** It's very unfashionable in modern-day America to talk about motherhood with respect to what it is women gain. We hear endlessly about what women lose, economically and professionally, when and if they drop out of the workforce to stay home with their children. But rarely do we hear about the unadulterated joys of motherhood. Nor do we hear about what children lose (more on this in the next chapter) by not having a parent at home. The subject is taboo. But I (SV) can tell you unequivocally that the smartest move I ever made was building a career around marriage and family rather than trying to build marriage and family around a career. It was an investment that continues to pay dividends to this day.

Skip the Shacking Up

Cohabitation in the U.S. has skyrocketed. Specifically, it has increased over the past half-century by *more than 1,500 percent*.[16] We can't think of a single other phenomenon that has occurred in such a short span of time and has been simultaneously embraced by the majority of Americans. "Living in sin," it appears, is in vogue. But here's what we know from the research: while cohabitation may not be harmful to marital longevity, there is *zero* evidence that it's helpful.

You won't be surprised to learn that those who are against cohabitation are primarily religious folks, for the obvious reason: it means unmarried couples are having sex. That is not our reason for discouraging you from shacking up.

Living together prior to marriage is simply counter-productive to lasting love—for several reasons. For one thing, just over 50 percent of first cohabiting couples ever get married. That means 50 percent of women waste their fertile years with men who will never commit.

Second, cohabiting couples have a separation rate five times that of married couples and a reconciliation rate that's one-third that of married couples. Finally, compared to those planning to marry, those who cohabitate have overall poorer relationship quality. They tend to have more fighting and violence and less reported happiness.[17]

But by far the biggest problem with shacking up is the one we never talk about: the psychological toll that moving in with someone, only to later move out, takes. It may be logistically easier (and cheaper) to separate after shacking up than it would be after getting divorced, but the emotional baggage people carry with them is often no less significant than had they been divorced. And if you've had multiple living partners, you can multiply the baggage. It's like getting divorced several times over. The ability to trust diminishes with each broken relationship, often until there's no trust left at all.

Just as important are the unique thought processes men and women go through when they decide to live together. Simply put, they don't match. Most women agree to live with their boyfriends because they believe it's a step toward marriage. But at some point, they become antsy. The insecurity of not knowing whether or not the relationship is permanent eats away at her. That's why the movie *He's Just Not That Into You* wasn't titled *She's Just Not That Into You.* It's typically the woman, not the man, who seeks lifelong commitment.

Men, on the other hand, are more likely to view shacking up as a means to test the relationship or to postpone commitment. "This gender asymmetry is associated with negative interactions and lower levels of commitment even after the relationship progresses to marriage," wrote Meg Jay in *The New York Times.*[18]

As if all that weren't enough, here are several more reasons we recommend you not live with a man to whom you are not engaged. One, *it does not allow for the objectivity you need in trying to determine whether or not he's "the one."* The reason the statistics on cohabitation make an exception for couples who are engaged prior to living together is that the decision about whom to marry has already been made. Conversely, cohabitating couples haven't made any decision at all. They're just playing house.

If you've already made the decision about whom to marry, moving in together prior to the wedding is not all that significant to the health of the marriage. But if you *haven't* made up your mind, if you're still deciding whether or not he (or she) is the one, living with him isn't going to help you decide. On the contrary, it will cloud your judgment. You'll get in deeper and deeper until eventually you can't see the forest for the trees. Living in separate spaces makes it much easier to make an informed decision.

The second reason is because *there's a psychological process that takes place once a decision is made.* Couples who approach their relationship assuming they'll be together until "death do us part" are very different from a relationship in which the end is unknown.

"The very option of being allowed to change our minds," wrote Barry Schwartz, "seems to increase the chances we *will* change our minds. When we can change our minds about decisions, we are less satisfied with them. When a decision is final, we engage in a variety of psychological processes that enhance our feelings about the choice we made relative to the alternatives."[19]

That's one of the reasons, perhaps the main reason, so many cohabitating couples don't make it to the altar.

Finally, there's this: while women pretend to be fine with shacking up, we don't buy it. Lack of commitment makes most women uneasy. Even if a woman appears content in her cohabiting relationship, more often than not she assumes the man she's living with is on the same page as she is as they move toward commitment and marriage. Her certainty about a long-term relationship is growing, and she assumes his is too. Sadly, she's often wrong.

It's not that men don't want to get married at all. But typically speaking, the longer they can postpone it, the longer many of them will. Men just aren't programmed to commit the way women are, although they can certainly be brought to the table. The best way to do that is to not shack up but to wait until he's certain he's ready and certain you're the woman he wants. And if that day doesn't come, move on.

There is just no upside to cohabitation. There are, however, many downsides. At the very least, it takes up valuable time you could otherwise be using to date marriage-minded men. As a woman, you only have so many chances to establish a serious relationship with a man, so it's costly to not be intentional about your love life. Those the months and years you spend in relationships that don't end in marriage are not only emotionally draining—you end up wasting valuable time. Your primary assets on the mating market, youth and beauty, will rapidly decline. But his will not.

And don't make the mistake of thinking fertility breakthroughs will allow you to have a family on your timetable. You'd have to be very rich to force those circumstances along, and it's not even desirable to do so. Having children late in life is very, very difficult. No one ever talks about that, but they should.

Consider Marrying Young(ish)

If you're at all a maverick, you might consider marrying earlier rather than later. That's one way to avoid hitting thirty with no man and no plan! By "earlier," we mean somewhere around age twenty-five. Any earlier than that and you run the risk of making a reckless decision. (If you want actual statistics, 60 percent of couples married between ages twenty and twenty-five end in divorce, and those who wait until they are older than that are 24 percent less likely to get divorced.)

We know you've been raised to postpone marriage indefinitely, but it's not working out very well. If anything, it has backfired. For one thing, finding a husband in your thirties is exceedingly difficult. Not only are the pickings slim, a woman's attractiveness peaks in her twenties. The same is true for men, except their power and status rises over time—which makes them more, not less, attractive to women. Women have their greatest bargaining power in their twenties. By the time they hit their thirties, they'll have to compete with younger, more beautiful women.

As countercultural as it is, **there are many advantages to marrying earlier rather than later**. One is that it's very helpful to have nailed down the most important decision of your life early on. It offers a lot of flexibility and plenty of time to focus on other things, whether it's building a career and/or saving money to buy a house or to allow one parent to stay home. I (SV) have a friend who married young and who waited *nine* years to have children! She and her husband enjoyed many years together unencumbered by the responsibilities of parenthood and saved a lot of money in the meantime.

Marrying earlier rather than later also gives you the option to have more than two children if that is what you want. It takes at least two years *each* to have and to recover from having a baby. So depending on how many children you want, you may need up to a ten-year period for this stage of life. At age thirty-five, your fertility will decline precipitously. So the ages of twenty-five to thirty-five are an ideal time to get married and have all the babies you want.

Marrying young(ish) also gives you the option to be a young mother. This alone has several advantages, such as a higher energy level (which you will need!) and ample help from grandparents while they're still active enough to help out. It's also helpful as far as having time in your life for both family and career, as there are many women who stay home with their children for x number of years and then later in life amp up their careers.

Perhaps the biggest advantage to marrying young(ish) is that you won't find yourself in the unenviable position of having to "hurry up and find a man to marry." This is a major problem with women who delay marriage and find themselves marrying whomever they happen to be dating (or even living with) to ensure they'll be able to have children. The entire dating process is undermined as a result of a ticking clock—you're just far less likely to choose well when you're under the gun.

So there are a lot of upsides to marrying earlier rather than later. Of course, if you were to float this idea around, you'll get a lot of pushback. Marrying later in life is the trend, and people don't like to buck trends. But in keeping with the theme of this book: just because something's popular doesn't mean it's good or even smart. Don't make that leap.

In the culture we live in today, it's almost always better to think outside the box—and this is particularly true when it comes to mapping out your life. Reject what the people around you tell you to do.

March to the beat of a different drum.

••

Principle 3

You can't approach sex and marriage the same way
a man can because your body has an agenda of its own.
Work with the biology you've been given.

••

4.

WHO WILL ROCK THE CRADLE WHEN THE BABY COMES?

WHEN I (SV) MET my husband, I was twenty-nine and he was thirty-three. I had been previously married (no kids), and he had not. Had I met my husband four years earlier, and had I been single, I never would have married him. In fact, I wouldn't have even gone out with him.

I met my husband late one Saturday night in 1997, in a bar of all places, after I'd moved back to St. Louis from New York. He had just come from a wedding and was wearing a suit with a striking blue tie. He was a big guy. And cute. And fit. Best of all, he was very easy to talk to. This was not the kind of guy who'd mastered pick-up lines. He just had a quiet, steady confidence about him.

That evening I learned that my yet-to-be-husband had received a master's degree in English with the intention of becoming a college professor; but after a short stint in academia, he ditched that plan and eventually moved into the business world. I also learned that we knew a lot of the same people, even though we were more than four years apart. He had attended an all-boys Catholic high school where my high school boyfriend had graduated; in fact, that's how our conversation started. At the end of the evening, my yet-to-be-husband gave me his card, took my number, and said he'd call.

He called that Wednesday night, and we talked for several hours without one awkward pause. We went on our first date that weekend—to dinner and a movie—and the rest, as they say, is history.

Now back to why I wouldn't have gone out with him had we met a few years earlier. After learning more about this nice, handsome man, it was clear he'd floundered throughout his twenties before landing on his feet professionally. And he couldn't help but notice that it had an effect on his love life. He knew that if he wanted to get married and have kids, he had to get serious about finding his way.

He ultimately did get serious, and it was several years later that I came along. As we got to know each other, it was clear that I wanted children and planned to stay home with them. Not only was he fine with that, he wanted the same thing.

Because of my plans to stay home, which were non-negotiable, I couldn't have—and wouldn't have—entertained dating a man who wasn't on a professional track. Ergo, when I learned what my yet-to-be-husband's life had been like in his twenties, I told him flat out that had I met him back then, I wouldn't have gone out with him.

He didn't blink. On the contrary, he understood. And that told me something. It told me he and I were on the *exact same page* when it came to the kind of life we wanted. And that made all the difference.

It's amazing to me that young couples today—especially the women!—skip this conversation during the dating process. But on closer examination, it makes sense. So much has happened in the past twenty years to make the topic of who will stay home moot. Or at least, *appear* moot. Many couples believe that living on one income, or even on one and a half incomes, is impossible to do. But if that were true, why do most families do just that? Contrary to popular belief, the majority of married couples with children under eighteen have mothers who are either not employed or who are employed part-time.

Less than half of all married mothers work full-time. That is typically because, when the baby arrives, and then a second baby or even a third, the enormity of the childrearing task comes barreling down on husbands and wives. And more often than not, the spouse who chooses to meet that enormous task is the wife. She may or may not work in some capacity outside the home, but she nevertheless chooses to make motherhood the center of her life.

The Alfred Kinsey studies, long known to be the most exhaustive research on human sexuality and sex differences to date, concluded the following: "The average female marries to establish a home, to establish a long-term affectionate relationship with a single spouse, and to have children whose welfare may become the prime business of her life."

Of course, many married mothers continue to work full-time outside the home, often because they assumed they always would and thus created a life that commands two salaries. That's what happened to Tina, a wife and mother of three young children. Listening to Tina talk about her life, it's clear she's in over her head. Like most women her age, Tina had absorbed the idea that "balancing" full-time work with young children is just what most women do. Thus, it must be manageable.

But her chaotic life proves otherwise. She and her husband must constantly decide who's going to take care of the kids on any given day, or who's going to schedule their work life in such a way as to accommodate the children. Moreover, Tina's children don't sleep on their own through the night and more often than not end up in their parents' bed. Finally, her son has serious behavioral problems. Unable to control him, Tina took him to a psychologist, whereupon he was diagnosed with oppositional defiant disorder, defined as a child who's "marked by defiant and disobedient behavior to authority figures."

Tina's son doesn't have oppositional defiant disorder any more than her children have a sleep disorder. Her children are suffering because, like many women today, Tina is trying to skip a crucial step of motherhood. The purpose of having a parent at home in the early years is to teach babies and toddlers how to sleep, eat, and behave—and to create an atmosphere that fosters the parent-child bond. This bonding is crucial for a baby's emotional development and allows parents to later discipline their children successfully because the trust has been established. If you skip this step, home can become a battlefield.

Naturally, Tina's convinced she and her husband can't afford to have one parent stay home, and that may very well be the case today, if they didn't plan in advance to live on one income. But what they have not considered is that it actually *costs* money to have a second parent working full-time since parents invariably outsource childcare, housework, and meal preparation. And that doesn't even include the costs of work attire, commuting, and eating out. You'd have to make a six-figure income for the arrangement to come out in the wash.

All of which is to say: **planning ahead for work-family arrangements is key**. There are myriad choices a couple can make *prior* to having children to ensure that staying home, at least in the early years, is possible. But women aren't encouraged to do this, so they don't. They just do what they think everyone around them is doing. They don't realize that most women aren't doing it, actually—no doubt because they underestimated the behind-the-scenes reality of such a life, as Tina is now experiencing.

It is critical that couples figure out *prior to marriage* how they're going to arrange their work-family lives. Women who are unsure about whether or not they will want to or will be able to stay home should know in advance about the rude awakening they'll have when they try to combine full-time work with mothering babies and toddlers.

There's a reason only a quarter of married mothers do it. And just because they're doing it doesn't mean they're doing it well.

The Wake-Up Call

We hear a great deal in the culture about how unfair it is that women take on the equivalent of two full-time jobs—the one outside the home and the one inside—while men don't have this same burden. In reality, women have chosen this path by creating lives that aren't conducive to motherhood. They didn't take into account the fact that they'd be out of the workforce for a period of time and have thus made motherhood downright painful.

Women also don't realize in advance that they're going to respond differently to motherhood than their husbands will to fatherhood. Women tend to take on the more emotional aspects of parenting. For example, you as a woman are more likely than your husband to hear the baby in the middle of the night. Or you may have trouble sleeping due to excessive worry over minor things you don't need to worry about. You may also be unable to relax enough to have sex with your husband once the kids are older. (It's much easier to have sex with babies and toddlers in the house than it is when they're older and know what you're doing.)

Conversely, most men will not react to every sound their baby makes and jump up to tend to him or her. Nor are they unable to have sex with their wives despite children being in the house. They're more likely to say, "Just lock the door!" These are just a few examples of the vastly different natures of men and women, which have a direct effect on the way they parent their children.

As a woman, you will be emotionally attached to your children in a unique and primal way. This should not be surprising: you're the sex that carries the baby in your womb for nine months! You're literally joined with your baby all that time, plus you're the sex that breastfeeds. Of *course* you're going to be a different kind of parent.

Women are just more sensitive to and concerned about the details of their children's care and emotional development than men are. While most husbands today are hands-on dads, wives tend to feel they can do a better job than men can in dealing with their children's emotional needs. And they are often right. Dads are as indispensable as mothers are, but a father's role tends to be more prominent when children are a bit older.

All of which is to say: the idea that men and/or society cause women to be unsuccessful at "balancing" full-time work and motherhood is both unfair and untrue. A man's response to the care of his children just isn't the same as a woman's. Remember my conversation (SV) with Katy? She and her husband haven't even *had* children yet, and she's already realized his thought process differs from hers. She wants her husband to feel equally angst-ridden about how they're going to fit kids into their lives, and he doesn't.

That's because she's a woman, and he's a man.

Our culture *is* to blame, however, for the way many mothers (especially new mothers) feel about their lives— but not for the reasons you think. It isn't because America doesn't offer paid family leave or adequate childcare, as feminists argue. It's because **America doesn't support or even *acknowledge* that women are unique to babies and children**.

"The drive to reproduce is instinctual, and the ability to nurture is in our DNA as women. But it must be turned on by the environment," writes veteran psychoanalyst Erica Komisar in her book *Being There*.[20] "Modern society is too often derisive toward women who embrace their biological tendencies, labeling them abnormal or unhealthy," she adds in an article for *The Wall Street Journal*.[21]

Indeed, there's a huge number of women today who would like to stay home with their children but cannot. They either assume that living on one income is impossible, and thus don't prepare financially in advance, or they assume children will fit snugly into their career lives and are shocked to discover how much work is involved in raising kids. It also doesn't occur to them that their husbands will react differently to parenthood than they will. They assume breadwinning and childcare can, and will, be split right down middle—as if neither sex has any unique proclivities at all.

The wake-up call is therefore loud and intrusive. Women often feel—I (SV) know because I've heard from them for years—as though they've been lied to. And they're right! They have been. That's why it's even more critical that couples determine in advance what our parents and grandparents never had to: Who's going to stay home with the kids? And if the answer is neither the husband nor the wife, who then? How is life going to work for the twenty or so years there are children in the home?

The potential for conflict with this still very new set of circumstances is huge—so huge it literally rips marriages apart. Knowing what kind of life you want when it comes to work and family is crucial, for it allows you to make the necessary arrangements in advance. Granted, the best laid plans don't always work out, but you can always modify or regroup. Either which way, you still need a plan. You need to know what kind of family life you want *before* you say "I do."

How old would you like to be when you have kids? How many children do you want? Where would you like to live? And whom you marry matters, for it will dictate where you end up. Some areas of the country are considerably less expensive to live, thus making it easier to live on one income if that is your goal.

Knowing what you want in advance can even affect the choices you make in college. Will you choose a college major or a career path that's conducive to motherhood or will you choose one that leaves no room for family?

It's true that not every woman knows in advance what she wants to do with her life or what she wants to do about the work-family dilemma. In that case, it's best to assume you *will* be out of the workforce for a time, not that you won't. Because it's much easier to reverse that plan than it is to reverse the other. Even if both you and your husband do end up working full-time after the kids come along, you will at least have left the option open to not have to do so.

At the end of the day, both you and your husband will rock the cradle. But one of you will rock it more, and the chances that that person will be you—and that you'll *want* it to be you—are high. And if your husband is the one who stays home, or if you outsource the care of your children to hired help, prepare to be walloped with a range of emotions that will upset the apple cart. **It is a rare woman who has a baby and happily and willingly relinquishes the motherhood role. That's not the message you receive from the culture, but the culture is wrong.**

You need to know in advance how strong the motherhood pull will be once you have children and thus plan to embrace it rather than avoid it. You will not regret taking care of your own babies, but you almost certainly will regret not doing so.

● ●

PRINCIPLE 4

Decide who will take on the lion's share of childrearing
and breadwinning tasks *before* you get married.
And don't even *think* of marrying a man who isn't
on the same page you are.

● ●

PART TWO

AFTER "I DO"

WE'RE GOING TO go out on a limb and assume that when you said "I do," you meant it. That is to say, we presume you didn't want to just *get* married. We presume you want to *stay* married.

We want that for you, too. Unfortunately, the safeguards that used to be in place to help couples maintain that goal—namely, social supports such as religion, premarital counseling, stricter divorce laws, and the like—no longer exist. What's more, positive cultural messages about men and marriage are gone. That makes staying married much more difficult.

To be perfectly frank, none of us has any idea what we're getting into when we say "I do." Forever is a very long time, and life as a wife bears no resemblance to life as a girlfriend. Well, it may at first. But ever so slowly—week by week, month by month, year by year—your relationship will begin its inevitable transformation. *That* is a guarantee.

I know women who've been married and divorced several times because they're addicted to the thrill of being in love: that newness, or that high we all get when we "fall in love." No relationship on the planet can sustain those feelings for the long haul. That's one of the reasons remarriages start out so seemingly well but eventually land in a ditch. Indeed, the divorce rate for second marriages is around 70 percent. Third marriages are even higher.

Love really is blind. During the initial dating stage, when you "fall in love," your brain releases a lot of dopamine that causes activities such as texting, talking, and kissing to feel amazing. In a way you could say that when you "fall in love" you become, temporarily at least, addicted to someone. At this point in the relationship, your man (or your woman) can do no wrong. If he does do something questionable, it's almost always rationalized in some way or assumed that whatever it is isn't that big of a deal.

This early stage of a relationship can go on for some time, but one thing's for certain: it has an expiration date. "The 'in-love' experience has a limited and predictable life span," writes Gary Chapman in his wildly successful book *The 5 Love Languages*.[22] "Eventually, we all descend from the clouds and plant our feet on earth again. Our eyes are opened, and we see the warts of the other person. Welcome to the real world of marriage."[23]

I (SV) was reminded of this the other day when I was getting a pedicure from my Asian friends at Tip O'Nails. Leanne, whose husband died some time ago and whose son is grown and gone, had "fallen in love" with a wonderful new man and was planning her wedding. She was so excited! For months she went on and on, as did the other ladies in the shop, about this amazing man she was about to marry. "He treat me good!" she said. "He perfect!" She was always smiling ear to ear when I saw her then.

That was about a year and a half ago, and the other day when I asked Leanne how things are with her new husband, her demeanor was noticeably different. It wasn't bad—nothing of concern had taken place. It's just that her response was far less animated. She said something along the lines of "Eh, he fine."

Clearly, the spell had worn off.

That the excitement of new love wears off may sound depressing, but it doesn't have to be—not if you change your perspective. Because as exhilarating as those early days are, what comes later is what truly fills the soul. "True love cannot begin until the 'in-love' experience has run its course," adds Chapman.

There are two great lines in *Away From Her*, a film about a couple who'd been married for decades when the wife gets Alzheimer's, that capture this sentiment perfectly. The first is when Fiona, the wife, says to her husband Grant, "I think people are too demanding. People want to be in love every single day. What a liability."[24]

The other is when Grant is talking to an aide at the memory care facility where Fiona resides. In thinking back to when he and his wife first met, he says, "It's curious, all that 'madly in love' business. I hear myself tell the story, and it sounds so crucial. But compared to what we ended up with, all that seems so superficial somehow."[25]

The love a married couple feels for one another after several decades is dramatically different from the love they felt for each other when they first met. But it's hard to know this if you're a product of divorce and have thus never seen long-lasting love, and when the culture in which you live celebrates "falling in love" but offers zero support and encouragement for what comes afterward.

The remainder of this book represents that support and encouragement. It offers the best possible advice we can to help sustain love for the long haul. It will allow you to begin your marriage with your eyes wide open or hit the rewind button if you're halfway in and need to reset the dial.

There's no reason for marriage to be a battlefield, and yet for so many couples that's what it has become—because no one wants to tell the truth about marriage, particularly as it pertains to gender and gender roles. No one wants to talk about the power of sex differences, and about how to navigate those differences for a lifetime.

But we have to.

Without that information, you're shooting blanks.

1.
WHAT IF EVERYTHING YOU THINK ABOUT MARRIAGE IS WRONG?

WHAT IF ALL YOU need to be successfully married is a change of attitude? Sound too good to be true? It isn't. You'd be surprised what a simple shift in thinking can do.

In fact, your attitude is the *single most important determinant* of your success in life, whether we're talking about your job or your marriage. Life will throw you a thousand curve balls. So will marriage. But it isn't the curve balls that matter—it's what you do with those curve balls. And what you *do* stems from how you *think.*

Here's what we mean. In a 2010 interview with Barbara Walters, the actress Sandra Bullock said, "I always had this feeling that if you got married, it was like the end of who you were."[26] And in the January 2019 issue of *Elle*, the twice-divorced Jennifer Aniston insists she doesn't need marriage and kids to be happy. "I'm sure, because I was from a divorced-parent home, that was another reason I wasn't like, 'Well, that looks like a great institution.'"[27]

No one is born with these thoughts—they are learned. Children of divorce have (understandably) had their belief in marriage shattered, and they tend to carry this belief with them throughout their lives. But beliefs aren't facts. They're learned assumptions based on observing marriages that didn't work. That doesn't mean the system is faulty; it means the individuals were. Your story can be different.

In order for that to happen, though, you must change the way you think. There is simply no way to sustain a marriage if your attitude toward the institution itself is negative or if it carries with it a suitcase of painful childhood memories. Bullock and Aniston's assertions speak volumes. Countless women today enter marriage with this exact same self-defeating mindset.

Every person who gets married brings with him or her a set of beliefs about marriage. These beliefs have more than one source, but there's no question our parents' model has the most impact. Children whose parents modeled what a successful marriage looks like have a huge leg up in life. The rest of us—which is to say, most of us—figure it out as we go along.

There's also the fact that **many women today had mothers who taught them to "never depend on a man."** That *says* something. It says that love doesn't last and that men can't be trusted. This mindset will land the marriage-minded woman in a ditch.

Just because your mother failed doesn't mean you will, too. But to succeed where she didn't, you'll need to reject everything you learned from her. <u>You'll need to decide that you do believe in marriage. And then marry a man who believes in marriage, too.</u>

That may sound obvious, but it isn't. Many people get married without ever discussing their beliefs on marriage as an institution. This is a mistake. Because if both partners don't share the same view of marriage, they won't approach what happens within the marriage in the same way. They'll be speaking different languages.

So what *are* your beliefs about marriage? What demons are you harboring based on what you saw and heard growing up and/or what you've learned from the culture? How much do you know about what marriage is and what it is not?

To find out, take this quiz.

The Quiz

Answer "True" or "False" to each of the following questions:

1. Love is all you need to make a marriage work.

2. Conflicts over money, sex, and housework are a sign that a marriage is in trouble.

3. If your husband loves you, he would know what you need and want. You shouldn't have to spell it out for him.

4. You should love yourself more than you love your spouse.

5. A wife shouldn't "settle" for less than she deserves.

6. Children should come before your spouse.

Now let's take a look at the answers:

1. Love is all you need to make a marriage work. (FALSE)

It's pretty much a given that when two people marry today, at least in the West, they're marrying for love. But if that were all that was needed to make a marriage work, most couples would stay together. In fact, love is only part of the equation. A necessary part, to be sure, but it is not enough. Respect is another key element, as are compatible goals, values, and realistic expectations.

This is where arranged marriages have a leg up. In arranged marriages, people expect that if the families of the bride and bridegroom are well matched, and the couple was brought up similarly to one another, they'll be compatible since they have similar beliefs about their roles and obligations. These couples don't expect marriage to be a perpetual date: exciting and romantic. They don't expect to feel "in love" with their partner all the time. And in expecting less, they receive more.

Not long ago I (SV) had a relationship coaching session with a Hasidic Jewish wife from Brooklyn, who later told me about an episode of *Oprah's Next Chapter* in which Oprah visits Hasidic Jewish families in Brooklyn. Oprah's interview with one family in particular mirrored what I learned from the Hasidic wife in my coaching session.

"You date only for the purpose of marriage, not for the purpose of having a fun time?" Oprah asked one of the two Hasidic couples she interviewed.

"Well, we have fun!" said the wife. "But the purpose of the date is to see if we're compatible."

"So, when you start dating, it's about shared values," Oprah asked.

"Definitely," said the husband. To which the wife added, "But you know what? The love that we share was never the goal. It's a byproduct."

"The love wasn't the goal?" Oprah asked incredulously.

"We don't get married for the purpose of love. We get married for the purpose of values, and the love is born from those values."

We in the West may scoff at the idea of marrying for any reason other than love, but we could stand to learn a thing or two from this practice. Did you know the divorce rate of Orthodox American Jews is roughly 10 percent, and the global divorce rate for arranged marriages is 6 percent? Ten and 6 percent!

The couples in these families know something we don't: **love is not enough to make a marriage work**. In fact, studies of marital stability show that loving feelings for a partner are more a *result* than a cause. Conversely, in non-arranged marriages (which is to say in most marriages), we often hear about couples "falling out of love." But there's really no such thing.

Marriages that are not arranged tend to end for one or both of two reasons: the wife no longer respects her husband or feels he doesn't give her enough attention, and/or the husband is sexually dissatisfied.

The various manifestations of this underlying issue are many: the husband works too much and is rarely home, or he *is* home enough but spends more time in front of the television than he does with his wife; the husband doesn't work hard or can't hold a job; the wife works too much so when she's home she's too tired for sex; one partner has an affair; one partner is an alcoholic; and so forth. But these are all just symptoms.

The cause is almost always that wife does not respect her husband (or doesn't show it), and the husband no longer showers his wife with love and attention. Couples often wonder which came first: the chicken or the egg? But it doesn't matter. At the end of the day, if they both concentrate on satisfying each other's unique desires—his need for respect and her need for love and attention—the couple is more likely to retain warm feelings for each other and will thus be more likely to stay together.

2. Conflicts over money, sex, and housework are a sign that a marriage is in trouble. (FALSE)

Did you know one of the greatest predictors of divorce is the *avoidance* of conflict? All marriages have conflict. Life is difficult and thus full of problems—why should marriage make us immune to this fact? If anything, marriage brings more conflict into our lives because we have to deal with two individuals' problems rather than one—plus the problems that come from trying to marry those two individuals' problems!

My husband's parents (SV) never fought and wound up divorced, whereas my parents fought constantly but stayed together. We're not saying fighting is good; we're just making a case for the research about conflict avoidance. The issue isn't whether a marriage will have conflict—it's how the couple should deal with the conflicts they face. What's the best way to approach problems without hurting the marriage?

Dr. John Gottman is a leading researcher in marriage who has done extensive work over four decades on divorce prediction and marital stability. His three main tips for dealing with conflict include: (1) explaining to your partner exactly what you need from him or her; (2) listening to your partner to try and understand his or her point of view; and (3) repairing your relationship when it isn't going well.

Some of this is easier said than done. It's hard to repair a relationship if the other person isn't willing to meet you halfway or cannot hear your point of view, for example. But that's where appreciating sex differences comes in handy. As a woman, you don't really need to *understand* your husband's needs—you just need to meet them. And as a man, you don't need to *understand* your wife's needs—you just need to meet them. If couples do this regularly and often, conflicts are fewer and far between.

Bottom line: it's not the existence of conflicts or problems that make or break a marriage. It's what you do with them that matters.

3. If your husband loves you, he would know what you need and want. You shouldn't have to spell it out for him. (FALSE)

It would be nice if men and women spoke the same language, but alas, they do not. Men are not mind readers—they need their wives to explain exactly what it is they want or need. If women are explicit in this way (as well as nice about it), their husbands will swoop in to do what is asked of them. It's in their nature to do so.

Problems arise when women think their husbands should "know" what to do, especially on the home front. For instance, you've probably read many articles by women that lament the fact that their husbands refuse to see what needs to be done at home. Wives don't want to have to ask their husbands to do it, nor do they want to be nice about it. They just get mad that their husbands don't see what needs to be done on their own and then complain about it.

It's much simpler to lay out what you want done— make a list if you have to—and to ask nicely. Wives are often reluctant to do this because the culture tells them they shouldn't have to. It's men who need to change their ways! Why should the wife have to tell the husband to do what he should already know to do?

You're welcome to take that approach if you want, but it will amount to beating a dead horse. Accepting men as they are and working within this framework is a much smarter, more peaceful, and foolproof plan to marital peace.

4. You should love yourself more than you love your spouse. (FALSE)

One of the trendiest ideas over the past few decades is the idea that people should love themselves. It's true that if a person doesn't feel worthy of love, he or she will have trouble expressing love and receiving it. So, in a sense it's true. But the initial concept has been blown way out of proportion.

You've been taught that how you feel about yourself is the most important thing, but it isn't. <u>The most important thing in a marriage is your ability to love another person *more* than you love yourself.</u> This goes against the status quo, but that's why so many marriages fail. Loving yourself more than loving your spouse basically means putting your own needs ahead of your spouse's. And that's a surefire path to divorce.

5. A wife shouldn't "settle" for less than she deserves. (FALSE)

One of many things that makes marriage so much harder today than it used to be is that women have been raised to believe they need to accept themselves just as they are and that they shouldn't have to change. "Never settle for less than the best!" you were told. "You *deserve* it." Consequently, women set their sights insanely high—which means one's husband will almost always appear subpar. It's inevitable.

High expectations are crippling to a marriage. In my last relationship coaching session (SV), I spoke with an unmarried thirty-something woman whose friends tell her to drop any guy she dates who has the slightest annoying habit. Over time, they said, his habits will become even more impossible to live with.

That these women have bad habits of their own didn't even occur to them. That's because they were raised to think they can do no wrong. This is a childish approach to relationships that will keep this woman's friends from ever being successful in love.

If you harbor a similar notion that you should never "settle" for less than the best, you are doomed to fail at love. You don't "deserve" anything—no one does. Erase that word from your vocabulary. It's part of the reason you're struggling.

6. Children should come before your spouse. (FALSE)

While it's perfectly natural for parents to make their children's well-being a priority, putting the needs of one's children ahead of the needs of the marriage is almost always bad idea. (One possible exception might be if you had a special needs child.)

Take Jeanne and Larry, for example. For Jeanne, the children always came first. She felt her husband Larry could take care of himself because he was an adult, and she rationalized her position by suggesting Larry wasn't focusing enough on the children and she therefore had to make up for that. Larry's position was that he didn't obsess about the kids because they needed to be able to stand on their own two feet. He felt Jeanne "babied" their kids.

It's extremely common for mothers to become overly focused on their children under the guise that their children "need" them in this way when, in reality, the women are avoiding the problems in their marriage. Or they don't want to look at the real reasons why they're using their children to fill the void they feel in their relationship with their husband.

"As time went by, it became obvious that having a child had fundamentally changed me," admits Lucy Cavendish at *The Daily Mail*. "The focus of my life became my child and not my partner. Whereas before I would maybe cook him dinner or meet him from work and go out, I spent all day with my son and then, later, I no longer had the energy to cook or chat into the small hours. Why should women put their husbands before their children? Husbands are adults. They can make their own decisions, earn their own money, they can even tie their own shoelaces."[28]

If you share this belief that a man can "do for himself" and that all your energies should thus be poured into your kids because well, they're kids, your marriage will be a ticking time bomb. Maintaining a healthy marriage is the single greatest gift you can give your kids.

• •

Principle 1

The attitude and beliefs you carry with you about marriage will determine which direction it will go.

• •

2.

THERE'S NO SUCH THING AS SEXUAL EQUALITY

IN *THE FUTURE OF MARRIAGE*, sociologist Jessie Bernard made the following observation: "I'm convinced that women and men are intrinsically so different that nothing we do will obliterate or even reduce the differences. I do not think men have to worry that women will become unsexed, or women, that men will. In fact, the freer we become in allowing both sexes to be themselves, the more the fundamental and ineradicable differences will show up."[29]

Almost fifty years later, Bernard's prediction has proven true. Men and women have never been freer to pursue the kind of lives they want. And yet, left to their own devices, they continue to make vastly different choices.

In Scandinavian countries, for instance, where the most has been done to achieve gender equality, sex differences have become larger, not smaller. In those countries, as in ours, there are significantly more female nurses than male nurses and significantly more male engineers than female engineers. There are also far more at-home mothers than there are at-home fathers.

Why? It's very simple. It's called biology.

Men's and Women's Brains

Over the past fifteen years, research on male and female brains has exploded. This has upset the apple-cart considerably, for the science now proves beyond a shadow of a doubt that there are undeniable differences between women and men that no amount of social engineering can undo.

For starters, men's brains and women's brains are organized differently. The right hemisphere is dominant in emotions, facial recognition, music, visual tasks, and identification of spatial relationships, while language skills are dominant in the left hemisphere. The brains of four-year-old girls show more advanced cell growth than do boys in the left hemisphere—and boys, more in the right hemisphere.

These anatomical sex differences are reflected in sex differences in language skills and spatial perception from a very early age. Men show a more definite separation of function between the two brain hemispheres and have a larger percentage of space in the right hemisphere devoted to visual-spatial functioning. Further, the corpus collosum—a large bundle of nerve fibers that joins and communicates between the two hemispheres—is larger and more bulbous in women.

There are thus two possible reasons for females having greater verbal access to their emotions. First, in men, more space in the right hemisphere is devoted to visual and spatial functions, leaving a smaller proportion of space for mediating emotions than in women.

Second, in women different functions are less localized and confined to one side of the brain because they enjoy better communication between the two hemispheres through the corpus collosum. For example, women with brain damage from trauma, epilepsy, or stroke are more able than men to substitute other areas of the brain to function in place of the damaged area.

All of these characteristics suggest the organization of the female brain is less rigidly specialized and localized than the male brain; this sex difference provides a basis for women's greater language skills, fewer speech and reading disorders, greater sensitivity to context and peripheral information, and greater access to emotion. Or, to put it in layman's terms: women are more intuitive, more in touch with their emotions, and more emotionally expressive than men are—and this sex difference has a biological basis.

Finally, there's a part of the brain called the hippocampus. Its main job is memory storage, and it is much larger in females than it is in males. Michael Gurian wrote about this in his books *The Wonder of Girls* and *The Wonder of Boys*. He used an example of a young boy and a young girl being asked by their parents to do three things around the house: clean up their rooms, take out the garbage, and wipe the table.

He said that more often than not, we will see the young girl complete the tasks with less reminding than the boy would need and that this has a lot to do with the hippocampal memory. Men are linear in their thinking. Generally speaking, they can only focus on one thing at a time.

Unfortunately, Americans have been conditioned to believe that the reason women do more housework and childcare is because their chauvinistic husbands expect them to—and that unless men start pulling their weight at home, women will never achieve equality. But most men don't *expect* women to do all the work at home. They just *don't care* whether or not the laundry gets done or the beds get made. That's a critical distinction.

Another big difference is sex. Sex takes up a lot of space in the male brain. Sex is a man's number one mode of communication—don't be put off by it just because it's different from yours. As a woman, you're more emotionally expressive and nurturing and, as a result, seek intimacy via cuddling, talking, and so forth.

That's not how it works for men. Men communicate via sex. Via *action*. Your husband isn't being insulting when you walk by and he grabs your butt. He's not being rude when he turns some innocuous statement you made into something sexual. He's trying to get close to you.

The best example of the difference between women and men when it comes to sex is this: how many men do you know who'd be offended if a woman told him she'd like to use his body for sex? Now turn that scenario around. If a man told a woman he'd like to use her body for sex, it would be grounds for sexual harassment. Apples and oranges.

Are "Equal" Marriages Even Desirable?

I (SV) share the second floor of an office building with two men, a father and a son, who sell insurance. We do not share an actual office, just a small kitchen and bathroom. I've only been renting it a year, but they've been there for years. And in all that time, I noticed, the kitchen and bathroom had never been cleaned. Not even once. As a result, I splurge on a housekeeper once a month to come and clean the common areas.

Another issue was the toilet: it was practically black inside as a result of the ceramic having been damaged by some sort of chemicals over the years. The black didn't come after several cleanings, so I asked the owner to replace the toilet, which he did. All of which is to say, the shared office space is much more pleasant. At least to me. Clearly my suite-mates couldn't care less.

This example may be a bit extreme, but the truth is that women simply care more about their surroundings than men do. Ergo, husbands and wives are not going to have the same approach about how and when to clean the house or how to decorate the house—nor will they necessarily agree on how to spend money on the home. And since women care so much more about their surroundings than their husbands do, they are almost always the first to notice what needs to be done.

The concept of "equal-partner" marriages—at least in the way it's defined by gender equality advocates, where husbands and wives become interchangeable, splitting the breadwinning, childcare, and household duties right down the middle—makes zero sense because it doesn't take into account the natural proclivities of women and men._

You may recall hearing about the American Psychological Association's (APA) new guidelines, released back in January, that deem traditionally masculine traits such as aggressiveness and stoicism "harmful." Author and professor Clay Routledge wrote this very funny satirical response to these guidelines:

> *With great shame, I have to confess that after some introspection I now realize the problem of traditional masculinity has taken hold of my own household. For years, I thought my wife and I were making division of labor and parental role decisions as equal partners and in a way that allowed us to balance as best we could our practical needs with our natural inclinations and interests. I thought my traditional masculinity and her traditional femininity were totally natural and healthy. Now I realize that we were both victims of a suffocating patriarchy. I am trying my best to get her to see the light but she may be beyond help. She still seems so happy and fulfilled. Maybe I should ask her to take some gender studies classes.*[30]

The idea that men and women can be virtually the same is not only preposterous but has proven not to be what most people want even if they *could* make it happen. And yet plenty of people give it a go. They embark on a so-called equal marriage under the misguided notion that the sexes are essentially the same.

Such was the case with Fred, a man I (JMT) interviewed a few years ago. At the time, Fred was a successful
thirty-eight-year-old divorced financial analyst. His
ex-wife was a very attractive doctor, and after Fred helped
get her through medical school, her earnings doubled his.
Here is Fred's story in his own words:

*Prior to getting married, my ex-wife and
I had a verbal agreement which stipulated
that she would maintain a low-profile career
and be supportive of my career. I had seen
other professional couples trying to match
careers and having difficulties with it. I knew
I wanted to take my own career seriously,
and I didn't think that there would be room
for two. At the time, she agreed.*

*After we moved, she started working in a
job she hated. She'd come home and complain
to me, and I felt bad for her. She was consid-
ering going back to school and getting a Ph.D.
in literature, but I insisted that all she would
accomplish is a lot of agony in grad school
and find herself jobless when she finished, so I
suggested she go to medical school. The more
we talked about it, the more she decided it
would be a good idea.*

*Before she entered medical school, she
worked, bought furniture, and baked bread.
She was cooking the meals. After she began*

school, I did the shopping, cooked all the meals, and did the vacuuming. We shared laundry, and she dusted. Gradually, I took on more of the household tasks. She was always in a crisis; she was terribly depressed and stressed. She was convinced that she was unable to come even close to measuring up to standards because everyone was much smarter and more capable. She was even afraid to speak up in class, so she began seeing a therapist for assertiveness training.

She did superbly in med school. At the end of her first year, she was first in her class. She didn't believe her grade report so she called the registrar to see if they had made a mistake. There was no mistake.

During this time, I felt like I was getting no support from her. I was going through a lot of stress. The people I was competing with were the best students from the best graduate schools. It was a level I never anticipated I would be in, and it was only getting more difficult by the day. I felt the crises she was bringing home were damaging to my career and to my peace of mind. The guys I was competing with were going home to supportive wives who didn't work or who had low-pressure jobs and who made a nice home and had a good time when their husbands were available.

I felt the relationship wasn't working out the way we had discussed when we agreed to get married, but I thought that it would be unfair to discuss this because she was going through a lot of difficulty herself, and I felt obliged to support her. I felt very strongly that she needed to do this in order to find a role for herself that was consistent with her abilities and needs. I saw it as an investment that someday, when she was fully trained and well-situated professionally, I would get the rewards of having a wife who remembered I helped her attain that. And I was willing to work at a job I hated in order to make it possible, but it was very costly. I wasn't getting anything out of it at all.

Fred's willingness to share household tasks did not make his wife more satisfied with him as a partner. In fact, as he helped to elevate her status and earning power, and reduce her vulnerability, he was damaging his own career and increasing his own vulnerability. As her status and earning potential sailed past his, his occupational status and paycheck became dispensable. He also became disposable as a mate since his wife was attractive and had a good chance of finding someone as good as or better than Fred. As it happens, such a man appeared—and Fred's marriage disintegrated.

There were several mistakes Fred made in his marriage—all because he projected his own male psychology onto his wife. At one point in their marriage, Fred and his wife (they did not have children) spent a year apart due to their respective careers, and during this time they each engaged in several extramarital affairs. Fred assumed that because *he* was capable of casual sex, his wife was, too, and her extramarital encounters would be as meaningless as his. That is not what happened.

Fred also assumed that once his wife's career was established, she wouldn't need so much emotional support from him. He didn't realize that women always need emotional investment from the men they love. These false assumptions led to Fred making decisions with his wife he otherwise would not have had he known how different men and women are.

Fred is not alone. **Countless husbands and wives have had their marriages fall apart due to the lie they've been fed that a good marriage is a union of "equals."** Not "equals" as in a partnership, the way you or we might think of it—equals as in *interchangeable*: as though husbands and wives can, and should, perform the exact same tasks with equal fervor and with identical results.

Where did such a radical idea come from?

It began in the 1960s, when feminist activists sold the idea that being a wife and mother traps women in a boring, degrading existence with many costs and few rewards, while men get to go out and lead exciting lives in the marketplace. That this narrative was terribly flawed, that it was politically skewed and devoid of common sense didn't matter. Feminists were shockingly successful in their goal, as they sold their message via the media for decades. It's really true that if you see and hear something often enough, it eventually becomes accepted as truth—whether or not it is.

Fast-forward five decades and a traditional division of labor in the household is now viewed as obsolete, reactionary, and oppressive, while dual-career marriages in which domestic chores and childcare are shared equally are viewed as normal, right, and good.

To be fair, the original criticism raised about traditional marriages was an inevitable reaction to the vulnerability of the mid-twentieth-century housewife, who was often saddled with many children and few modern conveniences. But those days are gone. Those who believe the 50-50 marriage is superior to traditional marriage make several assumptions— all unfounded.

The first assumption is that the old system was rigged against women or designed to oppress them. This is patently false. The traditional family unit was designed to *protect* women. Husbands were expected to take care of their wives financially since they bore, breastfed, and reared the children. Moreover, there simply wasn't time in the past for women to enjoy independent lives. Technology and reliable birth control hadn't come along yet to change all that.

In other words, it was nature, not man, that was oppressive—and both sexes were negatively affected. That's why husbands and wives worked together, doing the best they could to deal with far more challenging circumstances than couples do today. Watch a few episodes of *The Waltons* (or any other program that depicts life during the Depression or during wartime), and you'll come away with a very different view of gender roles than the one you've been saddled with your entire lives.

The second assumption is that marital division of labor is determined by husbands and wives' attitudes toward sex roles, and that a major determinant of these attitudes is the type of household in which they grew up. Individuals whose mothers did not work supposedly grew up with more traditional attitudes, and thus have a more traditional division of labor in their own marriages, whereas women whose mothers did work have more "enlightened" views of gender roles.

Contrary to this assumption, in my interviews with medical students (JMT), women whose mothers worked were in fact *more* willing to work part-time or to take time off from work while their children were small than were the women whose mothers stayed home. None of the women whose mothers stayed home said they would be willing to stop working completely, and most wanted to continue working full-time while their children were small.

It's likely that the women whose mothers worked when they were young felt slighted and thus don't want their children to have the same experience they did. And it is just as likely that the women whose mothers did stay home, but who don't plan to do so themselves, underestimate the amount of work and sacrifice their mothers made on their behalf. Down the road, when these same women have several young children of their own, they may very well change their minds.

My research also showed that sex-role attitudes do not predict how couples actually divide up household tasks. One study showed that <u>even women who considered themselves feminists did about as many household tasks as did more traditional women</u>, and all of these women did a lot more of these tasks than their male partners did.

In other words, there's no simple correlation between the values people are raised with or with their attitudes toward sex roles and their actual division of labor in adulthood. The idea that people reproduce their parents' marital roles, or that their attitudes toward sex roles determine their actual division of labor, are simplistic and misleading. Women tend to be practical about the sexual division of labor. Regardless of their sex-role ideology, if a man earns several times what they do, they do not expect him to wash dishes and change diapers when he gets home. If they do not want to perform these tasks, they can afford to hire extra help.

A third assumption is that wives and mothers who are employed are more satisfied with their marriages than wives and mothers who are not employed. On the contrary, some studies show that working wives are no happier than non-working wives; others show that working wives are *less* happy with their marriages.

It is true that working outside the home can increase a woman's satisfaction with herself. After all, earning a paycheck gives a woman more prestige and respect in the community and more bargaining power at home. As her earning power approaches or passes her husband's, she feels she has more right to demand that he take on more household tasks—and, in fact, research indicates she is more likely to have her demands met: the more a woman earns relative to her husband, the more domestic chores and childcare he is likely to perform.

But this woman is not necessarily happier with her marriage as a result of working outside the home because as her income and occupational status increases relative to her husband's, the total gain from his income and occupational status, over and above what she could obtain on her own, often declines. And we'll learn more in Chapter 4 about what happens when that is the case.

A fourth assumption is that husbands have nothing to lose by supporting their wives' careers: if men would simply shed their reactionary, chauvinistic attitudes toward sex roles, they would enjoy equal-partner marriages more than they enjoy traditional marriages.

This is demonstrably false. Men who perform more domestic tasks tend to experience *more* marital conflict and are thus more depressed. These husbands often envy men with better jobs whose wives do not work. It isn't men's attitudes toward sex roles that make them feel this way; rather, it's that when their wives work, men lose a good part of their support system.

Working wives simply have less time and energy for their husbands' physical and emotional needs and less time for domestic tasks. Wives with particularly demanding jobs therefore pressure their husbands to assume more domestic chores and childcare tasks. The result is that, while working wives gain status in society and bargaining power at home, their husbands lose in both arenas. The potential for conflict in equal-partner marriages is therefore very great.

And then there's the problem Fred had in his marriage: there's simply more opportunity—and more incentive, since partners aren't meeting each other's needs at home—to cheat when both spouses have high-pressure careers. In fact, when gender roles are completely inverted, when the wife is the main breadwinner instead of the husband, the husband is more likely to stray.

The culture will insist that's because men are threatened by their wives' greater earnings. But it's far more likely the husband is just lonely since his wife no longer has time for him. After all, if the wife outperforms her husband financially, she no longer respects him. And women don't want to have sex with men they don't respect.

The equality you've been taught to embrace suggests men and women are interchangeable, and they are not. A marriage can be reasonably fair—we say "reasonably" because nothing in life is fair, to anyone—without both partners living identical lives. Raising a family requires myriad tasks that make it very difficult for one person to navigate alone. If there's respect in the marriage, it shouldn't make any difference who's performing which task: who's earning more money, who's spending more time with the kids, who's doing more laundry and cooking, and so forth. If you start playing tit for tat, your marriage is doomed.

Moreover, how much work husbands and wives do on the home front depends upon several factors, such as which spouse is home more often. Whoever's home more is obviously going to do more of the work at home.

Problems regarding childcare and housework typically only arise when both partners work full-time and year-round—it is then that a marriage has the potential to become a war zone because the roles aren't clearly spelled out. Instead, there's constant negotiation. If both partners are leading identical lives, it's hard not to keep score. Conversely, couples who divvy up the household and breadwinning tasks by having each person in charge of a particular domain (which doesn't mean there's never any overlap) don't tend to keep score. Thus, they have fewer conflicts.

When you read articles or when you hear news reports about how husbands and wives divvy up the breadwinning, childcare, and household chores, what you rarely hear is that most women don't work outside the home at the same rate as most men. The distinction is important because, as we said, whoever's home more is naturally going to do more of the work in that domain. The notion that most women work the equivalent of two full-time jobs while men work only one job is a feminist fairy tale.

The average woman in America works twenty-six hours per week outside the home, and the average man works forty-eight. A study in the *Journal of Economic Literature* reports that while women perform roughly seventeen more hours of work inside the home, men perform roughly twenty-two more hours outside the home. When comparing the total amount of work men and women each do *inside and outside the home*, women average fifty-six hours and men average sixty-one.

My husband and I (SV), for instance, may appear to be a two-income household—and on paper we are. But my husband is the steady earner. How much I "work" depends entirely on where my children are in their development, both physically and emotionally. When they were babies and toddlers, I dropped out of sight completely. Now that they're both almost grown and gone, I've upped the ante considerably. In the interim, it was hit or miss. That's a fair representation of most families today.

In addition, those studies you read about don't take into account the work your husband *does* do at home; they just hone in on the diapers and the dishes. What about the gutters and the garage? The lawn? What about all the things that need tending to outdoors or in the basement, like the plumbing or the roof? What about transporting the kids to and from school or sporting events? What about picking things up at the grocery store on the way home from work? These are things most single guys don't do. They're things that come with the responsibility of being a husband and father, and the average man lives up to that task. In other words, both partners today are working equally hard, just in different locales.

At the end of the day, it's about teamwork. That's why the single most effective way to either jump-start your marriage or to improve it is to dump the concept of sexual equality. It has no business in a marriage.

● ●

PRINCIPLE 2

There's no such thing as sexual equality. It's sexual *in*equality, aka sex differences, that make marriage work.

● ●

3.

WHO *IS* THIS GUY I MARRIED?

WE OFTEN HEAR the adage "What do women want?" But we rarely hear (or even ask) about the inner workings of the male mind, or what it is *men* want. In previous generations, mothers passed on all kinds of advice and wisdom to their daughters about how to love a man. Their advice may seem quaint or passé, but it isn't. Because, while times may change, people don't. Human nature is human nature.

Unfortunately, there's a movement underway in America that not only questions male nature but seeks to eradicate it. This shift has been bubbling below the surface for years but came to a head with #Metoo and its subsequent assertion that masculinity is "toxic."

This gender propaganda has been incredibly harmful to both women and men. What makes it especially sad is that men, as a whole, are not only good but so easy to love it's ridiculous! All too often it's the refusal to love men, due to the resentment women have been groomed to harbor, that keeps marriages from flourishing. Put simply, <u>women have been conditioned to believe men suck</u>.

It's time to put these negative and self-sabotaging views of men in the trash, where they belong. All a good man wants is for his wife to be happy, and he'll go to great lengths to make it happen. He'll even support his wife's ideas, plans, or opinions if he doesn't agree with them. That's because a husband's number-one goal is to please his wife. If he determines his wife cannot be pleased, that's when the marriage is in trouble.

What a man wants in return for his devotion is respect, companionship, and sex. If you supply these basics, your husband will do anything for you—slay the dragons, kill the beast, work three jobs, and so on. Men will happily do this if, and only if, they are loved well in return. It is when men are not loved well that problems arise. That's how love works.

> Men, as a whole, are not only good but so easy to love it's ridiculous!

Now we know what you're thinking—that we're putting everything on you. Not exactly. Your husband is responsible for his own actions. If he makes stupid choices, it's his job to own up to them. What we *are* saying is that men tend to follow women's lead in love. Your husband's actions are more often than not *re*actions. He's reacting to something you said or did, or to something you didn't say or didn't do. He's reacting to your moods, your gestures, your inflections, and your tone. That's how men are. Your husband wants you to be happy, and when he sees it isn't working, he thinks he's failed. That's when he acts out.

To put it another way: a wife is in charge of the puppet strings. If she pulls on the wrong one, she gets a negative response. If she pulls on the right one, she gets a positive response.

Another way to think about it is to consider the game of chess. In chess, the king is the most important piece but also one of the weakest. He can only move one square in any direction—up, down, to the sides, and diagonally. The queen, however, is the most powerful piece. She can move in any one direction—forward, backward, sideways, or diagonally. And how *she* moves affects how he moves.

The key to any lasting marriage is to understand male nature and embrace it. If you don't do this, your relationship will be mired in conflict. Recognizing the sexes are equal but different removes all frustrations—"Why is he doing this?"—as well as the need to blame. There's no reason to get mad because you recognize and appreciate why your husband thinks and behaves as he does.

Masculine energy is different from feminine energy. Masculine energy conquers and cogitates. It likes to do things, and it likes to be alone to think about how to do those things. Feminine energy nurtures and verbalizes. It likes to talk, and to be pampered, and doted upon. That's why feminine energy is the receiver of masculine energy. It's why men should make the first move in a relationship—and why they ask the woman for her hand in marriage, rather than the other way around. As we wrote in Part One: the man acts, and the woman responds.

Now this next part is important: **That this is how the dance works doesn't mean men aren't** *capable* **of nurturing and that women aren't** *capable* **of conquering. It just means this isn't where each sex's natural energy flows.**

As you know, this subject has become wildly politicized due to the push for gender equality. Feminists repeatedly sell the notion that gender is a social construct, which means males and females only act as they do because of how they're raised. In fact, male and female nature is a deeply rooted part of evolutionary biology.

I (SV) was reminded of this when I passed my neighbor recently who was walking with her two young children, a boy and a girl. The baby girl was in a stroller, and her three-year-old brother was walking next to the stroller wearing a Superman costume. There was no party. It wasn't Halloween. The boy just wanted to be Superman. He wanted to be a hero.

When this boy's sister is his age, she will be much more likely to put on a princess costume, expressing her desire to be loved and cared for, than she will be to put on a Superwoman costume and pretend to conquer the world. She might put on a Superwoman costume, and that's fine. She might even wear both a princess costume and a Superwoman costume. But she is still *far more likely* to choose the princess costume. That is the reality of human nature.

It is true there's variation within the masculine/feminine framework—not every woman is 100 percent feminine and not every man is 100 percent masculine. There is overlap. But one thing is certain: masculinity and femininity are crucial for any relationship to last.

The film *My Big Fat Greek Wedding* demonstrates this sexual dynamic beautifully. Perhaps the most famous line is when Maria Portokalos, the family matriarch, tells her daughter Toula this about marriage: "The man may be the head of the household, but the woman is the neck. And she can turn the head *any way she wants*."[31] This positive and light-hearted approach to marriage is far more fruitful than a negative and resentful one.

Another example is when Toula gets excited about an opportunity to work at her aunt's travel agency and decides to broach the subject with her father, an old-school Greek who's obsessed with the idea of Toula marrying a Greek man and making lots of Greek babies. But Maria Portokalos knows the only way to get her husband to agree to Toula working at the agency is if he thinks it's his idea.

So, one day Maria, Toula, and the aunt are sitting in the family's restaurant with the dad, complaining about the aunt needing help at her agency and not knowing anyone who can do the job. The father says, "I know! Hire Nicky!" (Nick is his son, Toula's brother.) But Maria says Nick doesn't know how to use a computer. Then the three women pretend they have no idea what to do. Then the dad remembers that Toula has been taking computer classes.

So he says, "Aha! Toula can do it!" And Maria fawns all over her husband for coming up with such a great idea, as though she hadn't already thought of it herself.

There are loads of similar exchanges in *My Big Fat Greek Wedding* that teach great lessons about male nature, but you need a sense of humor to appreciate them. Many women today take offense at the idea that a wife should have to "cater" to her husband by appealing to his need to be right. But why argue with something that works? Why stomp your feet and complain it isn't fair when you could implement such strategies and move on with your day? It's much easier to work with what you've got than it is to try and move mountains.

Another (albeit frustrating) aspect of male nature is that a man needs to be "read." He's not going to come right out and tell you what he thinks and feels the way you do. Instead, you'll have to study your husband carefully.

Mothers of boys know this all too well. My son (SV) will not volunteer how his day went, nor will he share what he thinks or how he feels about something on command. He will, however, tell me when he's good and ready. And it's no different with husbands. This is largely due to the fact that men don't talk just to talk. They talk when there's something of value to say. We women, on the other hand, talk constantly—even when there's nothing to say!

Don't confuse a man's silence or simplicity with a lack of depth. Don't assume that because your husband doesn't express emotions the way you do that he lacks the ability to feel things. Men feel deeply, too. They just don't talk about their feelings every time they have them. They also don't react to their feelings as easily as women do. They keep them in check.

The Two Big Secrets of Loving a Man

There's a great scene in the movie *Annie Hall* in which a therapist asks the main character Alvy (played by Woody Allen) how often he and his girlfriend Annie (played by Diane Keaton) have sex. Alvy answers, "Hardly ever, maybe three times a week." Then the film, in a split screen, cuts to therapist asking Annie how often she and Alvy have sex, to which she replies, "All the time, like three times a week."[32]

The message couldn't be clearer: When it comes to sex, men and women have very different needs. These needs used to be something people understood and accepted. But in a culture that insists the sexes are "equal" as in *the same*, that understanding has vanished. As a result, so has any empathy for men's sexual desire.

But such empathy is crucial. Remember the young men in JMT's classes who explained that their reaction to visual images of women is automatic or programmed? That's what it's like to be a man. **Sex is their number-one mode of communication**. As a woman, you're more emotionally expressive and nurturing and, as a result, seek intimacy via cuddling, talking, and so forth. That's not how it works for men. Men communicate via sex. Via *action*.

Of course, not all men have the same sex drive. But most do, so unless you have reason to believe otherwise, you should assume your husband is like most men. Men. Love. Sex.

In the same way you need to talk, to *release* whatever's on your mind, men need a release of a different sort. But that release isn't just a physical act any more than your need to talk is just a physical act. When you talk to your husband and he gives you his undivided attention, that makes you feel loved, doesn't it?

It's the same way for him. Your husband wants to have sex with you because that's how *he* feels loved. And it's how he shows his love for you. If you hold this against him, or if you deny him the ability to show you his love, you're effectively telling him you don't love him.

We know that's not what you mean to suggest, but that is the end result. To turn your husband down in bed is akin to telling your husband you need to talk to him about something and his saying in response, "Sorry, not interested."

There's also the fact that getting your husband "in the mood" takes two seconds, tops. It's just an entirely different experience from a husband trying to get his wife in the mood. Women need to be warmed up. They need romance and candlelight and maybe a glass of wine. Think about how much effort you both put in to sex when you were first married—it probably went on all night! But once children come along, there are far fewer opportunities to set the stage "just so." Men like romance too. But they don't *need* it in order to have sex—that's the difference.

Which means when you're married with kids, there are going to be many times you're going to have to have sex whether you feel like it or not. If that sounds unpleasant, here's something to consider: the change in your husband's mood as a result of his having had sex with you is worth its weight in gold. He immediately shifts from being frustrated and irritable to being calm and conciliatory. You could ask your husband for just about anything at that point and he'd give it to you. It's not that different from the way you and I (SV) might feel after getting a foot rub or a massage. We're like jelly, and we're far more likely to say yes than we are to say no—to anything!

That's how it is for men and sex.

The second big secret to loving a man is one we touched upon in Chapter One: your husband's need for respect. Respect is the glue that makes your relationship work. Everything else, and I mean *everything* else, flows from there. In the same way you crave your husband's undivided attention, he craves your respect. If he has it, the relationship runs like a well-oiled machine. If he doesn't, it will die. And that's no exaggeration.

Yes, women want to be respected, too, and men want to be loved. But loving your husband comes more naturally to you than respecting him does—because that's *your* love language. And since respect is your husband's love language, he shows his respect better than he does his love. Men have to be taught and encouraged to love their wives, just as women have to be taught and encouraged to respect their husbands. Once they learn to speak each other's language, they see how much easier their relationships become.

Unfortunately, women are no longer encouraged to respect men; when you combine this trend with the fact that women are raised to rule the world rather than to be wives, it should come as no surprise that modern marriages fail. Since women are groomed to be in charge of men and to dismiss their husbands' needs, we've created a new sexual dynamic that undermines lasting love.

This is a major problem since husbands, as a rule, are inherently respectful of their wives. Men don't typically dismiss their wives' needs—on the contrary, men long to please their wives—or tell them what to do because men don't like to be told what to do themselves. Wives, on the other hand, seamlessly move from wife mode to mom mode once children come along.

That's almost always when an otherwise good marriage begins its descent. A husband doesn't want a mother, but too often that's exactly what he gets. A husband views being told what to do by his wife as disrespect. He thinks it means you don't believe he's capable of whatever it is you've told him to do—which, let's face it, you don't. That's why you're telling him how to do it. What happens then is that your relationship becomes imbalanced: he's *not* telling you what to do as a sign of respect, but you're not reciprocating. Over time, this wears the marriage down until there's nothing left.

Of course, wives who tell their husbands what to do don't view their behavior as a sign of disrespect. Many see it as "helping" their husbands be all they can be! Plus, a husband's behavior is a reflection of his wife, so she has a vested interest in what other people see when they look at her husband. Because of this, many wives consider it their *job* to lead their husbands in the same way they lead their children or in the same way they lead people at work.

But men don't want to be led.

Since your husband wants to make you happy, he will typically do whatever it is you want; but he doesn't want to be told when or how to do it. He doesn't want to feel as though you demanded it of him. That, to him, is a sign of disrespect. Rather, your husband wants to feel as though he chose to be of service to you, that he improved your life or made it immeasurably better or easier. And he's more likely to do that when he knows he has your respect.

At the end of the day, there are two ways you can approach men and marriage. You can say to yourself, "It's not fair that I have to steer this ship!" Or you can say to yourself, "Wow, so I hold all the power if I just learn how men think?"

The great thing about the latter is that a happy marriage is almost always within your control. If you chose a good man, you have the ability to create the kind of relationship you want. There's nothing stopping you except you.

So what are you waiting for?

• •

PRINCIPLE 3

Men are super simple. Cater to male nature,
and you can't go wrong.

• •

4.

BEWARE OF BEING THE BREADWINNER

Photo credit: Jonathan R. Corby

"Perhaps you should hunt, and I'll gather."

SUSAN FORRAY IS a forty-year-old divorced actuary and partner at a financial consulting firm who wrote in *The New York Times* about a man she had a relationship with who was unlike all the other men in her past, including her ex-husband, in that he believed in traditional gender roles. This gentleman told Ms. Forray flat out one day, "I'm the man. I should be in charge of the money."[33]

Ms. Forray felt a "jolt of anxiety."[34] Here she was, an *actuary*—that's someone who analyzes statistics and uses them to calculate insurance risks and premiums—and the man she's dating tells her managing money is *his* job, not hers.

"I found his bluntness surprising but also alluring. He was confident in his desires...I craved a man who sought to take financial responsibility for his family, even if I didn't need it.... The men I'd previously dated thought of themselves as staunch feminists—in hindsight, frustratingly so, at least in the sense that they were too inclined to defer to me (under the guise of respecting me) to ever take charge, either financially or sexually."[35]

Reading Forray's story made me think of Heather, a forty-year-old mother of two who lives in Colorado. She and I (SV) have exchanged emails for several years. Heather's husband considers himself a feminist and thus takes a more passive role in the marriage, preferring to have Heather be the breadwinner. Heather didn't see her husband's true colors, she told me, until after they'd had children, when he began to pursue his "financially unviable passions."

By "financially unviable passions," she means her husband's dreams of becoming a professional race car driver and snowboarder. When the pair first met, he was a retail store manager who merely dabbled in these passions outside of work. Heather assumed that if and when they married and had kids, those interests would come second to the demands of work and parenting.

She was wrong. Shortly after they married, her husband was laid off. It was the first of two layoffs post-marriage, as well as two prior to the wedding. "It seemed like with each higher level of 'need' in our family, he began excusing himself slowly from the responsibility of satisfying it. Instead of rising to the occasion, he began taking steps down from it."

Heather's husband began to spend more, not less, time on his hobbies. As a result, several years into their marriage Heather became the family breadwinner—a role she never wanted, and which has subsequently produced a well of resentment.

⚬⚬⚬

It is no coincidence that marriage and relationships have become more and more unstable as women have become richer and richer. Both the dating process and the marriage relationship have been unquestionably strained as a result of this phenomenon. Wealthy women have trouble in love—there's just no other way to put it.

It's actually rare now to come across a woman who *doesn't* make more than the man she's dating or the man she'd like to date. Yet these women have no appreciation for how significant this role reversal is, not just for men but for women as well. The research is overwhelming: neither sex likes it when the woman out-earns the man.

And when you think about it, it makes sense. Take a moment to consider the most significant difference between the sexes. It is women whose bodies have the ability to do something spectacular: carry life for nine months, give life, and nourish life. Their biology is also designed to nurture babies in a unique and primal way. A woman's value to society, in other words, is immeasurable—even if she never earns a dime.

That is not the case for men.

We're not suggesting men secretly long to give birth. We're saying a man's ability to provide for the life he helped create is integral to his identity. That's something he *can* do. Producing something of value for families and for society, as women do naturally, is how a man gets his sense of purpose. It is thus inevitable that if you upend this dynamic, the fallout is going to be huge.

Unlike a man, a woman's identity isn't inextricably linked to her ability to provide and protect. It's linked to motherhood. Any gynecologist can tell you that most women, if they haven't had children by their mid-thirties, become anxious. They cannot envision a life without children. No matter how committed they may be to their jobs, that desire is there. And when it's met, the woman's nurturing gene kicks in. Providing for that child emotionally, not financially, is her first instinct.

A man's first instinct is to make money, and a job or career is his means to do that. It's his unparalleled accomplishment in the same way that giving birth is to a woman. Ergo, when a man isn't providing for his family in a manner he deems satisfactory—meaning, if he doesn't make enough money to keep the family afloat, or if his wife makes more money than he does, or if his wife spends more than he's able to earn—he will not be happy. If by some miracle your husband could give birth tomorrow, wouldn't that take something away from you?

If you listen to the culture (which as you know, we don't recommend), you'll hear plenty of tripe about men not keeping up with the changing times. Women are breadwinners now; therefore, men should do "their part" by taking on more responsibilities at home, including raising the children.

There are two problems with that assertion. One, men are already taking on a tremendous amount of responsibility at home, three times more than their own fathers did. Two, most women don't want a full-on role reversal any more than men do.

According to Pew Research Center, in roughly two-thirds of married or cohabiting couples, men earn more than women. And the difference between the percentage of people who say men should be able to support a family financially and the percentage of people who say women should be able to support a family financially is striking: 71 percent to 32 percent, respectively.

These attitudes don't exist because Americans are sexist. They exist because most people understand that men and women are different physically and emotionally—that because women are the sex that gets pregnant, breastfeeds, and nurtures the babies, allowances must be made. Most Americans understand the reason for traditional marriage. It's only a small but vocal minority that does not.

> Most men have no desire to rely on their wives' incomes.

To bolster their argument for "equal" marriages, feminists and their allies insist that men are burdened being the primary breadwinners. But that just isn't true. Research shows, and biology dictates, that men view breadwinning as their responsibility. (There *are* some men who are willing to depend upon their partners' earnings, but few women find them attractive.)

Husbands may lament the pressures they face at work, but that doesn't mean they'd rather not work. Indeed, many men use the pressure to help propel them forward. Marriage tends to act as a stabilizer for men: they become motivated towards success when they know their families depend on them. A husband may like the extra income his wife brings home, and these days may even encourage her to work due to the high cost of living. But most men have no desire to *rely* on their wives' incomes.

Societal changes do not eradicate biological leanings.

In J. D. Vance's *Hillbilly Elegy*, the author writes about the poverty of his youth and the first time he felt "like a man." Growing up, Vance's "Mamaw," or grandmother, had been his savior from a mother who was strung out on drugs and who had an unfortunate habit of recycling husbands. When Vance was older and earned enough money to be able to help his Mamaw financially, he wrote that paying for her health insurance "made me feel, for the first time in my life, like I was the protector."[36]

Vance was also able to buy his family—his mother, his aunt, his grandmother, his sister, and her kids—Christmas presents, as well as take them to dinner. "To laugh and joke with the people I loved most," writes Vance, "as they scarfed down the meal that I'd provided gave me a feeling of joy and accomplishment that words can't possibly describe."[37]

To provide and to protect are at the core of a man's identity—whether it's 1919 or 2019. It is not his singular means to care for his family, but for him it's the most important. Thus, a man who is stripped of the ability to earn does not feel like a man at all.

And it's not just about how the husband feels. When a wife knows she can rely on her husband, irrespective of whether or not she's employed, her respect for him comes naturally. She wants to *feel* as though she's protected and provided for, even if she doesn't technically need him to.

That's why in the majority of American families with a married mom and dad and children at home, husbands make more than wives. In only one-quarter of these families does the wife earn more than the husband.

And when she does, the game changes. Why? **Because it isn't natural for the woman to be the dominant partner in the relationship.** No woman, deep down, wants to be in charge of her man. Every fiber of her being calls out for a man who's stronger and smarter and more capable than she. A man who can, and who will, take charge when necessary.

The moment a woman feels stronger or richer or more capable than her man, her respect and desire for him wanes. If this dynamic isn't remedied, a wife will eventually usurp her husband's role, and he will take a step back to accommodate her. At some point, the sex will stop, and the relationship will die.

This, by the way, is typically why men marry women who are less educated or who makes less money than they do. There's no competition! It's also the reason highly successful women often wind up alone. Think of all the really powerful women you know of. Now count how many are married.

"So what are you saying?" you ask. "That we should all back to the days when wives didn't work and were financially dependent on their husbands?"

No. But nor should we assume that women have it better today than women did "back in the day" just because they're richer. In reality, women have robbed Peter to pay Paul. They may be richer and more powerful, but they are also alone.

And if they aren't alone, they're exhausted and resentful from taking too much on. They're saddled with guilt and stress from being wives, mothers, and full-time employees—which women "back in the day" never felt. They also secretly crave a man who takes financial responsibility for his family, whether they need him to or not.

In other words, women threw out the baby with the bath water. It's one thing to encourage people to think outside the box with respect to gender roles—we should all strive to be flexible—and quite another to say biology is bogus.

The million-dollar question isn't "Do we go back?" but "How do we move forward?" How can women be economically independent and still find lasting love?

The answer to that question depends on another question. What do you want? When you think about your life, what is it that you want above all else? You need to know the answer to this. If the most important thing is to have a rock-solid marriage and to raise healthy, happy kids, then that has to be the priority. Everything else needs to fit in around that.

If, on the other hand, the most important thing is to become a doctor or a lawyer or an actress or a politician, or to pursue any career that takes up the majority of your waking hours, then *that's* the priority. You cannot succeed at both of these goals simultaneously because careers and relationships both take time to build and to maintain. When you focus on one, the other is invariably neglected. That's the nature of choice.

Just as the at-home mom or dad loses ground at the office, the career-focused parent loses traction at home. These two domains don't actually blend at all. They collide! That's why the work-life "balance" women are always seeking continues to be elusive. And it's why moms and dads who have distinct roles fare better than those who play catch-as-catch-can. It doesn't work to have two people piloting a plane. You need one pilot and one co-pilot to get the job done.

A great plan for women that is rarely discussed (since women are supposed to live their lives the way men live theirs) is to choose a career that has a lot of flexibility, thus allowing you to have a stress-free life at home. Because the bigger your job is, the more you're going to struggle—with your marriage *and* with your kids.

"Don't forsake relationships and family and children for your job. It's not worth it. It will never be worth it," wrote former CEO of Lehman Brothers Erin Callan Montella in *Full Circle: A Memoir of Leaning In Too Far and the Journey Back*. "It will inevitably end in disappointment. It has to. Keep those priorities in the forefront as you try to live a happy and productive life. Make choices that are consistent with those priorities. Pursue career paths that allow for the roles you want those priorities to play in your life."[38]

To be clear: we're not suggesting you not pursue a big career if that is what you want to do. We're merely pointing out the risks you take in choosing to do so. It's no accident that many highly successful women wind up single or divorced. Success has a price tag, for women and for men.

Several years ago, I (SV) watched a documentary on the rock band Journey. In it, Ross Valory, one of the band members, reminisced about the early days of the band's success. Here's what he had to say: "A lot of people don't know what the price is when they step up to the plate. The wear and tear is a mental and emotional thing. You really just let go of a lot of relationships that require presence and constant nurturing. You say goodbye to people. People get sick and die when you're gone, and just a lot of things go by the wayside."[39]

At that point in the interview Valory began to tear up. In fact, several of the band's members—including Steve Perry, the lead singer, and guitarist Neal Schon, who's been married five times—have talked openly about how success destroys love. They even convey this message in their songs.

What Women Really Want

In 2006, *Forbes* staff writer Michael Noer took a lot of heat for his article entitled "Don't Marry Career Women." In it, Noer highlighted research that found both men and women are unhappy when wives make more money than their husbands. "A recent study in *Social Forces* found that women—even those with a 'feminist' outlook—are happier when their husband is the primary breadwinner," he wrote.[40]

Unfortunately, the culture we live in today encourages women to ignore a man's salary because a woman is supposed to take care of herself rather than rely on a man. But getting a good education and developing a skill for the marketplace, which every person should do, does not supplant maternal desire. Most women have children, even if they put it off. And when they do, they won't have the option to stay home unless they married a man who's a steady earner or who's in a position to become a steady earner.

Nor will they have this option if they made financial decisions based on two incomes instead of one. Or if they ignored, or more likely didn't know because no one told them, the psychological toll their financial success would have on their marriage.

Take Karie, who conveyed the following to me in an email:

> When I was growing up, my mother stressed the importance of getting a good career as a woman. Her father, my grandfather, had died when my mom was in her teens and left my grandmother with nothing. The family struggled. My mother never forgot the experience and strongly encouraged us children to become independent in all ways. I believed this message. It seemed sensible to me to be able to take care of myself.
>
> Today I am forty years old, and I make $350,000 per year as a physician. My husband works at home on our farm. It may sound like an ideal situation, but this role reversal has caused enormous conflict. I am jealous of the fact that he gets to stay at home, and he is jealous of the fact that I get to go to work. I lack respect for him because I'm bringing home all the money.

I regret that I'm not an at-home mom and wife, supporting my family instead of leading them. I leave the house at 4:30 a.m. and get home at 6:30 p.m. I am too tired for sex at night. My husband tries to lead, but I take charge because I am the breadwinner. When a woman is the breadwinner, she feels it is her right to lead the family. The feminist message is so strong. We are all influenced by it. It is not good. It is not right.

Stress and jealousy are two big factors that upset the equilibrium when the husband is out-earned by his wife. If the gender roles in Karie's marriage were reversed, if she was home and her husband was the physician, he would not be plagued with the feelings his wife has about the arrangement. If he had been the physician and Karie had stayed home, they'd be swimming with the tide rather than against it.

Karie's story represents why, statistically speaking, the happiest marriages are those that are more traditional in nature. This does *not* mean a wife never works outside the home, nor does it mean a husband isn't a hands-on dad. It just means the husband is the steady earner and the wife takes on the lion's share at home.

Beth is another great for example. Beth is a fifty-three-year-old, twice-divorced mother of three children. She has an MBA from a prestigious university and is uber-ambitious. Her most recent venture, real estate, has been her most lucrative endeavor. Most real estate agents are not what you'd call off-the-charts successful: the majority net around $30,000 per year. Top-tiered agents, on the other hand, are very successful. As in, they make far more money than I suspect even they anticipated. Beth falls into the latter category.

At present, Beth is dating and hoping to find a match—but it isn't easy. She clearly doesn't "need" a man for either financial or procreative reasons. Moreover, at her age, the pickings are slim. She likes the man she's dating now very much, but he's already expressed ambivalence about the amount of money Beth makes relative to him.

Beth's second marriage ended because she was the dominant partner. Her earnings far exceeded her ex-husband's, and at one point, Beth had even encouraged him to come work for her. Big mistake! No man wants to work for his wife. *With* her, possibly, but not for her. And while that's how Beth presented it and indeed viewed it herself—as the two of them working together—her ex clearly did not. After all, Beth built the business from the ground up; he had nothing to do with it. He *would*, in effect, be working for her. And very few men want to do that.

I (SV) have a friend who knew I was writing this book and told me about a friend of hers who has a high-powered job and who's married to a man who works part-time and is responsible for the after-school life of their school-aged kids. It sounds like an ideal arrangement: the couple is very wealthy as a result of the wife's job, and the kids are well cared for. But the couple attends a great deal of marriage counseling to hold their marriage together. My friend's friend is not emotionally satisfied with her husband and in response has chosen to "recalibrate" her expectations of her husband and her marriage in order to avoid divorce.

The common thread in relationships like these—where the wife out-earns the husband—is the lack of sexual chemistry. A woman's need for a strong, competent man on whom she can rely is directly related to her desire for him. Susan Forray learned this during her brief relationship with Traditional Man, the gentleman who told her he should be responsible for the finances. "I relish being cared for. He was fiscally responsible, generous, and trustworthy. So I told myself there was nothing wrong with the man being in charge of the money as long as he makes good decisions."[41]

She then told a story of how Traditional Man had fought off a dog who had attacked his son—and said that's what she loved about him. "Given the choice between a man who said all the right things about supporting a strong woman and a man who shielded his child from a vicious dog with his bare hands, I choose the latter."[42]

Having a man who's physically strong and on whom you can rely—financially and otherwise—is a prerequisite for a strong sexual relationship. That's the theme of almost all great love stories, and even Disney films such as *Beauty and the Beast*. The woman longs to tame the beast by channeling male lust and love in her direction.

It's an age-old theme that goes back decades. The one and only time viewers saw the strong-willed Scarlett O'Hara truly happy in *Gone with the Wind* was the morning after her husband Rhett dragged her up to their bedroom in a drunken state and made mad, passionate love to her. Today we call this marital rape. Back then it was called hot. Even the most successful, ambitious women long for men they can't dominate and fear their success may prevent their finding such a man.

Biology matters. Most women just aren't attracted to a man who doesn't earn a living or who makes considerably less than they do. To give you an idea of just how strong this primal need is, consider a comment a woman named Chris made on my (SV) blog:

> When we were first married, I made more than my husband and for a few months, I was the sole provider. Thirty years later I've been a stay-at-home mom of six children, and we have truly loved our traditional roles. But my husband has been ill for several years, and while I understand the challenges he faces, his illness has made his masculinity less masculine and it's affecting everything from how he parents to how he performs as a husband. It's been definite proof that a strong man is what our family thrives on, and I'm uncertain how to help my husband regain the respect he so desires and deserves.

This might strike you as unkind. In reality, Chris is pointing out the uncomfortable fact that an idle man, even if he's physically unable to be productive, is a lost man. He feels powerless. And it's hard to be attracted to a powerless man—women aren't made to respond to that sexually. It doesn't mean a woman can't love or care for man who's unproductive. But her respect and her desire for him will wane.

Bottom line: <u>If a woman feels as though her husband can take care of the family financially should she hypothetically stop working, she feels safe. If, on the other hand, she feels duty-bound to produce an income for the sake of the family, she'll very likely be restless and unhappy.</u>

Most married women who work outside the home do so because they want to, not because they feel a primal need to protect and provide for their families. This is in part what causes so much angst and conflict in dual-income marriages. Husbands and wives are both working, but they work for different reasons and are thus not "equal" in their approach to work and family.

In Forray's analysis of her relationship with Traditional Man, she insists that having a man's man and a feminist man aren't "mutually exclusive." But they are. Women can either have a man who offers strength and protection, or they can have a man who suppresses that part of his nature because he's been told that that's what women want.

That is not what women want. That's what women have been *told* they want. Or should want. There's a difference.

We recognize that some of this is hard to swallow. To suggest traditional sex roles are good and, to a large degree, fixed, isn't popular. But the evidence suggests they are. Women, as a rule, continue to marry across and up the dominance hierarchy for two reasons: because they need a man on whom they can rely once the children come along; and because it's simply sexier to have a strong and competent husband. This sexual yin and yang is crucial for any relationship to thrive.

Indeed, a 2012 study showed that when men perform more traditionally feminine chores—such as cooking, vacuuming, and laundry—the couples had sex 1.5 fewer times per month than those with husbands who did more masculine chores. And it wasn't just how often the couples had sex. The more traditional the division of labor, the more satisfied the wife was sexually.

Accepting the reality of male and female nature and its relationship to breadwinning doesn't mean wives need to quit their jobs. It just means that women who have their own money need to understand how these circumstances affect their marriage or relationship and make the necessary adjustments: work less, perhaps, or make a career change that's more conducive to marriage and family.

If the suggestion that you curb your work goals to accommodate family offends you, ask yourself why. It's possible you've placed too much stock in your career. It's possible your identity is too wrapped up in what you do rather than in who you are and in whom you love.

That may very well be why you're struggling.

PRINCIPLE 4

The happiest marriages are those
that are more traditional in nature.

5. TAKE DIVORCE OFF THE TABLE

HAVE YOU HEARD that quippy answer to the question, "What's the secret of a long marriage?"

Don't get divorced.

There's a lot of truth to that. For one thing, the decision to simply never divorce no matter what (barring abuse or addiction) leaves all the room in the world for the marriage to improve over time, which it typically does. Time does wonders for perspective. One study by the Institute for American Values showed that "two out of three unhappily married adults who avoided divorce reported being happily married five years later."[43] This was true even after controlling for race, age, gender, and income.

Here's another great reason to take divorce off the table: it's contagious! Research by sociologist James H. Fowler found that if a sibling divorces, we're 22 percent more likely to get divorced ourselves. And when our friends get divorced, it's even more influential: people who had a divorced friend were *147 percent* more likely to get divorced than people whose friends' marriages were intact.

One hundred and forty-seven percent!

In light of such research, what are some things you can do to keep divorce at bay? We will answer that question in the rest of this book, but the first thing you must do is take divorce off the table. Pretend it isn't an option. Just as we wrote about shacking up, knowing you can always get out of something will directly affect the amount of effort you put into it. To reiterate Barry Schwartz in *The Paradox of Choice*, "When a decision is final, we engage in a variety of psychological processes that enhance our feelings about the choice we made relative to the alternatives."

This psychological process applies to any choice we make. Whether you're deciding which car, television, or jeans to buy, or whether you're deciding whether or not to stay married, make your decision as though you have no options. We cannot stress the significance of this attitude enough.

Once you've made your choice to stay, just know and accept that you're going to have problems—big problems, problems that may cause you to question why the heck you married your husband in the first place—but that divorce isn't the answer to those problems. If you can do that, you're well on your way to a successful marriage.

Not long ago, I (SV) had a conversation with a sixty-something wife and mother named Sally. Sally has been married to her husband for forty-four years, and when I asked her what she thinks the problem is with the modern generation—why they can't get the marriage thing right—she didn't hesitate. "They don't know what a vow is." Everything is disposable today, she said. If something isn't working, people throw it out.

There's no question that we live in a throwaway society, and this absolutely affects our relationships. The environment in which we live matters, just as who we surround ourselves with matters. We are all connected.

Here's an idea to get you thinking differently about marriage. The next time you hit a rough patch, pretend you and your husband are stranded on an island. Assume that in order to get off the island you have to work things out, and see if this doesn't change the way you approach your relationship. Clearly, you're not stuck. The point is to do the psychological work that's necessary to stay together.

When people get divorced and remarry, unless the first choice was exceptionally bad (and certainly that happens), they typically end up with the same bell curve of happiness. This is in part because more often than not, people who get divorced don't change their thinking when they remarry. That's one of the reasons second marriages are more precarious than first marriages. (And third marriages are more precarious than second, and fourth marriages are more precarious than third…) People need to find their "sweet spot"—determine what they can live with and what they cannot—or their relationships will never last.

Remember: doubting your choice in a mate is perfectly normal. People tend to believe that couples who stay married must be really happy all the time, as if they don't have the same trials and tribulations as couples who get divorced do. As if happily married couples spoon together every night in bed and never fight. But as we learned in Part Two, Chapter 1, one of the greatest predictors of divorce is not the existence of conflict but the *avoidance* of conflict. So, the next time you see those couples who never argue, don't be envious of them! They could be headed for trouble.

The second-best way to avoid divorce is to lower your expectations! Women's standards today are completely unrealistic; they simply want too much. No one man can fulfill all your sexual and financial desires, *plus* make a great husband and father who's home all the time doing childcare and housework, *plus* fulfill all your emotional needs. You have to decide what's most important and move it to the top of the list. Stop expecting marriage to provide something it can't.

Men don't have this same burden because their needs are far more simple. All they want is to find a nice woman who's pretty, who treats them well, and who likes sex. That's about the sum of it. In fact, have you ever heard the joke about the husband store?

>So there's this store in New York City called The Husband Store, where women can go to choose a husband. At the entrance to the store is this sign: "You may visit the store ONLY ONCE!"
>
>Inside, there are six floors, and the men's value increases as women ascend each flight of stairs. They are permitted to

choose any man they want from a particular floor, or they can choose to go up another floor. They cannot, however, go back down except to exit the building.

So, a woman goes into the store to find a husband. On the first floor the signs says, "These men have jobs." On the second floor, the sign says, "These men have jobs and love kids." On the third floor, the sign says, "These men have jobs, love kids, and are extremely good looking."

Wow, the woman thinks. This is great! Nevertheless, she keeps going. She goes to the fourth floor, and the sign there says, "These men have jobs, love kids, are drop-dead good looking, and help with the housework."

"Mercy me!" the woman says, "I can hardly stand it!" Yet still she goes up to the fifth floor. And the sign there reads, "These men have jobs, love kids, are drop-dead gorgeous, help with the housework, and have a strong romantic streak." The woman is tempted to stop there, but she doesn't.

Instead she goes to the sixth floor, where the sign reads, "You are visitor 3,261,496,012 to this floor. There are no men on this floor. This floor exists solely as proof that women are impossible to *please. Thank you for shopping at The Husband Store."*

To avoid gender bias charges, the store's owner opens The Wife Store just across the street. On the first floor are wives who love sex. On the second floor are wives who love sex and who are kind. On the third floor are wives who love sex, who are kind, and who enjoy sports.

The fourth, fifth, and sixth floors have never been visited.

Pretty funny, right? Because it's so *true*. Men, as a rule, are easy to please—which means their expectations of marriage aren't inflated. Even if your husband does expect something, he's far more likely to hope you deliver than he is to expect or demand that you deliver.

Men are practical, too. They accept that when they make a decision, that's it—the decision is made. They don't fantasize about what could be or should be. They just live. It may be hard to get a man to the altar; but once he's there, he's pretty much settled.

Women tend to hold out for the fairy tale. They focus on the "what ifs" rather than on the "what is," and this attitude undermines their success in love. Then, when their marriage doesn't fulfill their unrealistic expectations, they think divorce is the answer. Here's a paragraph from an article entitled "Confessions of a Semi-Happy Wife":

> *Beneath the thumpingly ordinary nature of our marriage—every marriage—runs the silent chyron of divorce.... Thank God for divorce, which may be the last-standing woman's right to choose.... One eloquent swing of the ax and happiness is thrust firmly back into our own hands.*

It is impossible to overstate the significance of messages like this one. It means when you hit a wall in your marriage, and you will, the culture won't offer the support you need to climb over it. Instead, this is what you'll get: if you're not happy, leave.

Talk about sabotage! Who's never unhappy? And why should becoming a wife (or a husband, for that matter) guarantee one's happiness? Yet this directive—"life's too short; move on if you're unhappy"—is pervasive, and it's tailored specifically to women.

To be clear, we're not saying divorce isn't sometimes necessary. But we live in a culture that equates divorce with liberation, rather than as a last-ditch solution for extreme circumstances. Ask any honest psychologist, and he or she will tell you that divorce is a temporary relief at best. More often than not, **divorce creates more problems than it solves**.

Not only does divorce hurt children, as well as the relationship parents have with their children, most people who get divorced go on to remarry and thus bring with them the same unresolved issues from their first marriage.

That's because the problem wasn't necessarily the marriage but the way the couple dealt with the problems in that marriage. A new marriage will present just as many problems as the old. More, in fact, if children are involved.

Divorce, in other words, is no panacea. If you truly want to avoid it, remove it from your mind altogether. A recent survey of 1,000 married women showed 50 percent of women—50 percent!—have a "backup husband," or a man who serves as Plan B in case their marriages fail. Talk about undermining your own marriage! These women have created a self-fulfilling prophecy. Fantasizing about a marriage that doesn't exist and preparing for the demise of your actual marriage will almost certainly lead to its death.

It's your attitude that makes the difference. The way we handle conflict when we assume we'll be together "til death do us part" is very different from the way we approach conflict when we assume we can always leave. "The very option of being allowed to change our minds seems to increase the chances we *will* change our minds. When we can change our minds about decisions, we are less satisfied with them," writes Schwartz.[44]

That's why mentally removing the option to divorce is a great strategy for staying the course. Instead of wasting time thinking about what could be, or what you think could be if you were only married to the "right guy," you'll be focused on the guy you already have and will learn how to be happy with him. Because if you think you won't eventually end up in the boat you're in now with somebody else, think again.

PRINCIPLE 5

Take divorce off the table,
and you set the stage for success.

6.
NEVER, EVER DO THIS ONE THING

LYNN, THIRTY-EIGHT, WAS UNHAPPY in her marriage. Her husband was a great husband and father, and he made a good living. But Lynn was bored. She wanted the excitement of something new, and she wanted to be married to a wealthier man. After several affairs, Lynn finally found what she was looking for and divorced her husband to marry her rich boyfriend.

Life was good for a while—not for the kids, obviously, who saw much less of their father and who missed him terribly, but for Lynn. She enjoyed the perks that came with being married to her new husband.

What Lynn didn't foresee, or conveniently over-looked, was the flipside of the equation. While the man Lynn married was wealthy on paper, he was also a party boy who never grew up. An alcoholic, he lived primarily on his parents' money, and he didn't hold a candle to the caliber of Lynn's first husband, whose character was unparalleled. Lynn's new marriage lasted, but barely. And not happily.

❦

There's an underlying thought process many married women harbor, either consciously or subconsciously: that they can do better. That somewhere out there (or already waiting in the wings) is a man who doesn't have her husband's faults. Someone who is more exciting, more loyal, sexier, more loving or more caring. But most divorcées find their new partners have many of the same faults their old partners did, or they have different but equally serious flaws.

For instance, women with financially successful husbands often complain that their husbands don't communicate enough or spend quality time with them; while women whose husbands are caring and available are more likely to complain that their husbands don't make enough money. Indeed, a woman's ideal mate is something akin to Brad Pitt and the boy next door all rolled up into one.

Finding that man is like finding a needle in a haystack. For one thing, there just aren't many men like that. Moreover, if they do exist they've already been snatched up. The vast majority of women will need to accept the inevitable trade-offs of whatever choice they make. Men (or for that matter, women) with super successful careers will likely preclude large amounts of family time. Conversely, family men usually aren't rich.

Many women I interviewed (JMT) had satisfactory marriages but left them for the lure of what they thought would be a better investment, only to find that the men they desired were unwilling to marry them or had much less to invest than the women had originally thought.

One woman left a young, successful lawyer who was reliable but "dull and boring" for a man who promised a glamorous life of sailing, travel, and affluence. This man turned out to be a dreamer who had deluded himself—and her—into thinking he had the potential to become a great architect. He never became an architect, had a nowhere job, and ultimately depended on her ambition and income to attain a comfortable standard of living. She divorced this man and regrets leaving her dull, boring, but devoted and stable first husband.

Josie, a thirty-year-old Mexican American, reports a similar experience:

> *My first husband was patient and considerate. I would come home tired from work and complain and put him down, and he would just accept it. We shared all the household chores 50-50. I managed the budget and paid the bills. We hardly ever had disagreements. Anything I did was okay with him.*
>
> *Our friends were shocked when we split up because they had thought we were the ideal couple, but I think I would have done better with someone more aggressive. He was too soft, too easy, too mellow; he didn't have the drive to go anywhere. He*

had gone to college but was satisfied to work the graveyard shift in a warehouse. I felt he could have done better.

The man I'm with now is different. I met him in a club where he was playing in a band. He was very aggressive and persistent in trying to get me to go out with him. He acted very caring and affectionate at first. He was much more macho and sexy than my husband. But now that we're living together, he's not affectionate at all. He says he needs his space and I shouldn't bother him. We hardly ever do anything together. He's an artist and musician and wants to do his own thing, but he doesn't have a steady income.

I feel pretty crummy about breaking up with my husband now. He didn't want to split up. He was good to me, but I wasn't satisfied. Now he's got a girlfriend and is going to marry her, and I'm jealous. I made a mistake leaving him.

It isn't always the wife who makes this mistake; sometimes it's the husband. Joe, thirty-two, had three children, a loyal wife, and a stable marriage, but he felt he was missing out on life. He had a fantasy of what the single life would be like: driving a sports car, dancing at discos, and meeting young, sexy women with whom he would have a string of torrid sexual experiences. He also thought that if he ever wanted to settle down again and get married, he could easily do so with someone more attractive and exciting than his wife.

His fantasy did not materialize. Life in singles bars was bleak and unrewarding. The women he found attractive rejected him. Even the women who were no more attractive than his wife didn't respond positively to Joe.

Joe missed his children and the security of home life, and the divorce settlement and child-support payments didn't leave him enough money to live the kind of life he had envisioned. When he finally reconciled with his wife, he underwent a religious conversion and became deeply involved in Catholicism. He's now an exemplary family man and says that he's truly happy for the first time in his life.

I (JMT) encountered numerous individuals in my anthropological research who had left stable relationships, spent some time in the dating market, and suffered from the rampant competition and situational morality they encountered. In some cases, the experience of being "burned" caused a religious or moral transformation: they just decided to no longer chase unrealistic fantasies and to look instead for a good solid partner with whom they could establish a secure and comfortable life.

Three of the married couples I interviewed had previously been separated or divorced and had gotten back together. In each case, their reconciliations were accompanied by religious transformations that involved the establishment of rules and understandings concerning marital duties and obligations.

The success of these couples' new marriages seemed to depend on three factors: a rock-solid commitment to staying married (in other words, divorce was no longer considered an option); mutual agreement on their respective obligations; and more realistic expectations of marriage, as well as of the improbability of finding better partners.

Green Grass Syndrome

Green Grass Syndrome, or the idea that there's a person or a life "out there" somewhere that's better for you than the one you already have, is toxic. If you don't fall prey to it, you are significantly ahead of the game. Because unless you're being mistreated, nothing "out there" is better than what you have now. Different, yes. But not better.

We know this is much easier said than done. We know it's human nature to compare one's life to what you think others have that's better than what you have. But doing so will throw a grenade on your marriage. Nothing good can come from it. When it comes to choosing a husband, your best course of action is to decide what you need — let's call them your "non-negotiables" — and forget about the rest. Because the man you marry, no matter who he is, is going to have flaws. And guess what?

So do you.

What makes this hard to accept is that the modern generation of women has been raised to think they're perfect just the way they are. You don't have to *do* anything to be important anymore—you're important just for being born. "Never settle for less than the best!" you were told. "You *deserve* it." Consequently, you've set your sights insanely high. Which means every potential mate is going to appear substandard.

The best thing you can do for yourself and for your marriage is to become a "satisficer." A satisficer concentrates on the reasons she made the decision she did and practices gratitude for the wisdom of that choice. Now if your choice of husband was wildly stupid—you married a man who's prone to abuse and addiction, or who can't hold a job, or who lacks character—that's one thing. But assuming you didn't do this, focus on why you chose the man you did. Focus on what he brings to the table and be done with it. Don't look for more.

You're simply better off staying with the husband you've already chosen, assuming he's safe and if children are involved. It is infinitely easier to improve an existing marriage than it is to start over from scratch. Because give it enough time, and that marriage will have just as many warts as the first. What will you do then? Become Drew Barrymore?

We're not suggesting divorce is never the answer. It may be. What we're saying is that divorce is never the answer *if the purpose is to find happiness with someone you think is better*. Your happiness is not dependent upon anyone but you. Moreover, the happiness you think you might have with someone else is built on a fantasy. It isn't real.

Leaving one relationship for another is no guarantee of a better life. A spouse will often pursue a new and exciting relationship in order to escape the problems in the current relationship, only to end up with problems of a different sort in the new relationship. People get caught up in the moment and forget that over time, things won't seem so exciting anymore.

"The feeling of ecstatic lovingness that character-izes the experience of falling in love always passes. The honeymoon always ends. The bloom of romance always fades," writes M. Scott Peck wrote in his wildly successful 1978 book *The Road Less Traveled*. "We must be committed beyond the boundaries of the self."[45]

Unfortunately, this is not a worldview espoused by today's culture, which makes Green Grass Syndrome all the more difficult to avoid. At some point in your marriage, you and your husband will face some very real problems; it is then that you may find yourself questioning your choice of a husband. And when that happens, if it happens, you may start to notice other people's husbands. You may think to yourself, *Gee, why can't my husband be like that?*

That's when you need to stop. Don't go any further. And remember: you can never get everything you want all wrapped up in one man. No matter whom you marry, if you're a victim of Green Grass Syndrome, the grass will always look greener on the other side of the fence. But these things you're noticing, whatever they may be, only seem greener. In reality, the grass on that other side is just as brown as it is on yours. *Assume* this is true (because it is), and you'll quickly get your mind off other people's lives and put it back on your own, where it belongs.

This is where so many women get into trouble. The culture in which we live encourages women to search for something better when they're dissatisfied. We're not saying the average woman treats her marriage with little regard. We're saying when the going gets tough, and it will, the culture in which we live helps push you out the door.

You need to understand that when doubt creeps in, it doesn't mean your marriage is doomed, and it doesn't mean you chose the wrong husband. Everyone has doubts. Doubt is normal. Human. But it doesn't have to be debilitating. In order to avoid this fate, you need a firm understanding of Green Grass Syndrome.

And then you need to reject it.

● ●

PRINCIPLE 6

The key to a successful marriage
(and for that matter, to a successful life)
is to be happy with what you have
rather than to pine for what you have not.

● ●

CONCLUSION

FOUR FINAL THOUGHTS

Part Two of this book is designed to help you have a happy, healthy marriage—assuming you put the advice into action. Having the right attitude, rejecting the concept of sexual equality, understanding the male mind, not being the major breadwinner, having an unwavering commitment to marriage, and avoiding Green Grass Syndrome are, from both a research and a practical perspective, the best divorce deterrents.

That said, here are four final thoughts on marriage with which we'd like to leave you:

1. Accept that your own faults, along with some of your partner's, are permanent.

Of the many couples I (JMT) spoke with who'd been married more than twenty-five years, most felt that one of the most difficult things about living with someone was accepting the fact that that other person has his or her own perspective, opinions, and peculiar habits, and that many of these traits never change. They said too often people marry with the idea that their partner is more or less okay but needs a little working on, that their partner will eventually see the light. It is far more common for women to harbor this mindset.

But very often the pet peeves that were there at the beginning of the relationship are still there twenty years later—only now they're more annoying because the romantic passion, the naivete, and the novelty of their relationship is no longer there to mask these traits. Accepting your partner for who he or she is can be difficult, but even more difficult is recognizing your faults and having the insight and humility to realize that your style and habits are at least as challenging and annoying to your partner as your partner's are to you. Remember at the beginning of Part Two when I (SV) wrote about a conversation I had in my last relationship coaching session with a thirty-something woman whose friends all tell her to drop any guy she dates who has the slightest annoying habit?

Yeah, that's what we mean.

2. Recognize each other's sexual and emotional needs and build them into the way you live.

Male-female differences are persistent and tenacious, and as a result, conflicts are inevitable. I (JMT) interviewed a couple recently who was at complete odds about their sex life.

The husband thought his wife didn't understand that he really wanted sex, and he also couldn't understand why she didn't want to do it. I asked the wife whether it was true that she did not understand that her husband wanted sex and that it was very important to him. She said she understood perfectly, but she didn't want to do it as often as he wanted. The husband found his wife's attitude incomprehensible. Why wouldn't she just go ahead and do it? He really wanted it, it would make him feel good, and it wouldn't take very long.

But of course, to enjoy sex a woman has to get in the mood; and it's not always easy for her to put herself in the mood unless the conditions are just so. How to solve this problem?

Men need to recognize that women can't get aroused at the drop of a hat the way men can. They need to be romanced or "warmed up." That doesn't mean a husband has to take his wife out for a candlelight dinner every time he wants to have sex. But it might mean lighting some candles or putting on some soft music, or it might mean giving his wife a foot rub. Basically, husbands would do well to consider how they *used* to romance their wives at the beginning of the relationship and repeat those actions as often as they can.

For their part, women need to recognize that men don't need a perfect mood setting or even foreplay. Therefore, just as husbands will occasionally go out of their way to set the stage for sex, wives will sometimes need to have sex when they don't initially feel like it. It's a trade-off.

3. Make sure you like (not just love) the man you marry.

This may sound obvious, but you'd be surprised how many people marry someone they love but don't necessarily like. Forever is a long time, and we can't count on our loving feelings to see us through. Feelings change. You're not always going to feel warm and fuzzy about your husband (and he certainly won't always feel warm and fuzzy about you).

But if you *like* him—genuinely like spending time together, the way you do with your friends—that will sustain you. It's far more important for longevity's sake that you like your husband than it is for you to get goose bumps every time you look at him. That's the dominant feeling we all get in the early stage of a relationship, but it's not going to be the thing that gets you through. Liking each other will.

4. Don't have a fancy wedding.

Did you know the average—average!—cost of a wedding in America today is $33,391. Indeed, twenty-first-century weddings are big business. Church weddings with banquet hall receptions are out, and fancy destination weddings are in. Even weddings in one's hometown are elaborate. That tells you all you need to know about our culture's shift in values. Marriage is no longer viewed as a spiritual or even a serious endeavor. It's a party, pure and simple.

Of course there are exceptions to the rule, but attend the average wedding today, and they all have a similar feel. Whether or not a lot of money is spent, the climate is roughly the same. For starters, there are no priests or pastors officiating the ceremony. Instead, couples are married by their friends and family members who've been ordained as ministers *online*.

When I (SV) witnessed this for the first time, I didn't understand. "Who's that person marrying so-and-so? He looks just like the couple!" I asked my husband. Or: "Wait, what's so-and-so doing marrying our nephew?" Eventually I caught on, and all I can say is this: I understand that religion has taken a nosedive and that as a result couples don't even know a member of the clergy they can ask to officiate at their wedding. But let's be honest: something huge is lost when your friends and family can marry you. It's almost like couples are pretending to get married rather than actually getting married.

Fancy weddings say something profound: they demonstrate right from the get-go that couples are approaching marriage the wrong way. In 2014, a study by two economics professors at Emory University found that couples who spend less on their wedding tend to have longer-lasting marriages than those who splurge. It also found a similar correlation between less-expensive engagement rings and lower divorce rates.

The report concluded that couples who spend $20,000 on their wedding—excluding the cost of the ring—are 46 percent more likely than average to get divorced.

Conversely, those who spend between $1,000 and $5,000 are 18 percent less likely to split.

It makes sense when you think about it. Presumably, the couple who spends a lot of money on their wedding is more focused on getting married—on having a party—than they are on the spiritual nature of marriage. In other words, they're entering marriage with the wrong attitude, or perhaps they're getting married for the wrong reasons.

Conversely, the couple who spends less on a wedding (or who has a more understated wedding without all the fanfare) will not only have more money to put toward establishing a life together, they're probably more focused on the meaning of the event than on the event itself.

I (SV) can personally vouch for this. When I was twenty-three, I married the wrong man for the wrong reasons and was uber-focused on the wedding. I didn't spend anything close to the average amount people do today, but the year was 1991, so it might come out in the wash. That marriage lasted four years (no kids), and when I finally remarried, some three years later, I did things very differently. It was still an elegant affair, but it was much smaller and thus less expensive. And I pulled a dress off a rack for maybe a hundred bucks.

When I think about both of my weddings, I can clearly see the difference in my attitude with each event. The second time, I wasn't that invested in the wedding. I remember feeling happy to be gathering with the people I love, but I was much more interested in what came after: getting on with my new life with my new husband.

Granted, I had the first experience with which to compare the second, and I remember wanting to do everything opposite of the way I did things the first time. Even so, I could be the poster child for the above study since my first marriage ended and I've been married to my second husband for over twenty years.

Just something to think about.

ENDNOTES

A Note from John

1. Jordan Peterson, interview by Cathy Newman, Channel 4 News UK (January 16, 2018).

Part One: Before "I Do"

2. Kate Julian, "Why Are Young People Having So Little Sex?" *The Atlantic*, December 2018, https://www.theatlantic.com/magazine/archive/2018/12/the-sex-recession/573949/.

3. Chris Donahue, "Oscar-winner Chris Donahue Returns Home to USA Film Festival for Latest Project," online video clip, *Good Morning Texas*, WFAA, 26 April 2017.

1. Stop Trying to Have Sex Like a Man

4. Miriam Grossman, M.D., *Unprotected: A Campus Psychiatrist Reveals How Political Correctness in Her Profession Endangers Every Student* (New York: Sentinel, 2007), 3.

5. Kerry Cohen, *Loose Girl: A Memoir of Promiscuity* (New York: Hyperion, 2008), 3.

6. Cohen, 10.

7. Victoria Bekiempis, "Weinstein's Rape Accuser Said 'I Love You' After Alleged Attack, Lawyers Say," *The Daily Beast*, August 3, 2018, https://www.thedailybeast.com/weinstein-lawyer-dismiss-charges-because-he-had-consensual-intimate-relationship-with-alleged-victim?ref=author.

8. Jennifer Joyner, "I Thought Casual Sex Would Be Empowering, but It Was the Opposite," *Verily*, February 3, 2016, https://verilymag.com/2016/02/hookup-culture-sex-feminism-sexual-freedom.

9. Elizabeth L. Paul and Kristen A. Hayes, "The Casualties of 'Casual' Sex: A Qualitative Exploration of the Phenomenology of College Students' Hookups," *Journal of Social and Personal Relationships* 19, no. 5 (October 2002): 639–61.

10. Heather Mac Donald, "Policing Sexual Desire," *City Journal*, January 14, 2018, https://www.city-journal.org/html/policing-sexual-desire-15669.html.

2. Master These 8 Dating Rules

11. Nina Totenberg, "O'Connor, Rehnquist And A Supreme Marriage Proposal," *Morning Edition*, NPR, October 31, 2018, https://www.npr.org/2018/10/31/662293127/a-supreme-marriage-proposal.

12. Jordan Peterson interviewed by Jay Caspian Kang, VICE News, February 7, 2018.

3. How *Not* to be 30 with No Man and No Plan

13. Danielle Crittenden, *What Our Mothers Didn't Tell Us* (New York: Simon & Schuster, 1999), 25.

14. Julian, "So Little Sex."

15. Julian, "So Little Sex."

16. Meg Jay, "The Downside of Cohabiting Before Marriage," *The New York Times*, April 14, 2012, https://www.nytimes.com/2012/04/15/opinion/sunday/the-downside-of-cohabiting-before-marriage.html.

17. Sheri Stritof, "Essential Cohabitation Facts and Statistics," *The Spruce*, February 1, 2019, https://www.thespruce.com/cohabitation-facts-and-statistics-2302236.

18. Meg Jay, "The Downside of Cohabiting."

19. Barry Schwartz, *The Paradox of Choice: Why More Is Less* (New York: Harper Collins, 2004), 228.

4. Who Will Rock the Cradle When the Baby Comes?

20. Erica Komisar, *Being There: Why Prioritizing Motherhood in the First Three Years Matters* (New York: Tarcher Perigee, 2017), 166.

21. Erica Komisar, "Masculinity Isn't a Sickness," *The Wall Street Journal*, January 16, 2019, https://www.wsj.com/articles/masculinity-isnt-a-sickness-11547682809.

Part Two: After "I Do"

22. Gary Chapman, *The 5 Love Languages: The Secret to Love That Lasts* (Northfield Publishing, Reprint 2015), 21.

23. Chapman, *The 5 Love Languages*, 30.

24. *Away From Her*, directed by Sarah Polley, performed by Julie Christie and Gordon Pinsent, Capri Releasing, Echo Lake Productions, and Foundry Films, 2006, film.

25. *Away From Her*.

1. What if Everything You Think About Marriage Is Wrong?

26. Brad LaRosa, "Sandra Bullock Ribs Street on Rivalry: 'I'm Gonna Beat the S*** Out of Her!'" ABC News, March 4, 2010, https://abcnews.go.com/Entertainment/

Oscar_Stars/sandra-bullock-barbara-walters-oscar-special/
story?id=10002538.

27. Carina Chocano, "Jennifer Aniston Doesn't Need a Happy
Ending," *Elle*, December 7, 2018, https://www.elle.com/
culture/celebrities/a25426565/jennifer-aniston/.

28. Lucy Cavendish, "Why I'll Always Put My Children Before
My Husband… Even Though It's Already Destroyed One
Relationship," *The Daily Mail*, April 5, 2010, https://www.
dailymail.co.uk/femail/article-1263575/Why-Ill-children-hus-
band--destroyed-relationship.html.

2. There's No Such Thing as Sexual Equality

29. Jessie Bernard, *The Future of Marriage* (The World Publishing
Company, 1972), 256.

30. Clay Routledge, "Thank You, APA," *Quillette,* January 23,
2019, https://quillette.com/2019/01/23/thank-you-apa/.

3. Who *Is* This Guy I Married?

31. *My Big Fat Greek Wedding*, directed by Joel Zwick, performed
by Nia Vardalos and John Corbett, Gold Circle Films, 2002,
film.

32. *Annie Hall*, directed by Woody Allen, performed by Woody
Allen and Diane Keaton, United Artists, 1977, film.

4. Beware of Being the Breadwinner

33. Susan Forray, "How I Fell for an 'I'm the Man' Man," *The
New York Times*, October 26, 2018, https://www.nytimes.
com/2018/10/26/style/modern-love-im-the-man.html.

34. Forray, "How I Fell."

35. Forray, "How I Fell."

36. J. D. Vance, *Hillbilly Elegy* (New York: Harper Collins, 2016), 167.

37. Vance, *Hillbilly Elegy*, 167.

38. Erin Callan Montella to Melissa Langsam Braunstein, "From Wall Street Hot Shot to Wife and Mother," Institute for Family Studies, May 10, 2016.

39. *Don't Stop Believin': Everyman's Journey*, directed by Ramona S. Diaz, performed by Arnel Pineda and Neal Schon, HBO, 2012 documentary.

40. Michael Noer, "Don't Marry Career Women," *Forbes*, August 22, 2006, https://www.forbes.com/2006/08/21/careers-marriage-dating_cx_mn_0821women.html.

41. Forray, "How I Fell."

42. Forray, "How I Fell."

5. Take Divorce Off the Table

43. Linda J. Waite et al., "Does Divorce Make People Happy? Findings From a Study of Unhappy Marriages," Institute for American Values, 2002, http://americanvalues.org/catalog/pdfs/does_divorce_make_people_happy.pdf.

44. Barry Schwartz, *The Paradox of Choice: Why More Is Less* (New York: Harper Collins, 2004), 228.

6. Never, Ever Do This One Thing

45. M. Scott Peck, *The Road Less Traveled* (New York: Simon & Schuster, 1978), 85.

ABOUT THE AUTHORS

Suzanne Venker is an author, columnist, and relationship coach known as The Feminist Fixer. For over fifteen years Suzanne has freed women from feminist attitudes that hurt their relationships and undermine their ability to find lasting love. Her writing has appeared in many publications, including *The New York Post*, *USA Today*, *Time*, and *Parents*. *Women Who Win at Love* is her fifth book.

Visit www.suzannevenker.com to learn more.

John M. Townsend, Ph.D., is Professor of Anthropology at Syracuse University and an expert on the evolutionary roots of sex differences. He has authored countless articles, as well as the book *What Women Want—What Men Want* (Oxford University Press), and has appeared on many national television and radio talk shows.